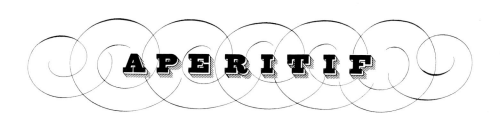

APERITIF

D1031418

CHRONICLE BOOKS · SAN FRANCISCO

Georgeanne Brennan

APERITIF

RECIPES FOR SIMPLE PLEASURES IN THE FRENCH STYLE

Photographs by Kathryn Kleinman

STYLING BY ETHEL BRENNAN

To my dear friends Georgina and Denys Fine — Georgeanne
To my husband, Michael Schwab, for his newfound love of aperitifs — Kathryn

Text copyright © 1997 by Georgeanne Brennan. Photographs copyright © 1997 by
Kathryn Kleinman. All rights reserved. No part of this book may be reproduced in any
form without written permission from the publisher. Gerald Hirigoyen's recipe for
Wild Mushroom and Goat Cheese *Galettes* is from his book *Bistro* and is published
with permission from Sunset Books and Weldon Owen, Inc. Library of Con-
gress Cataloging-in-Publication Data: Brennan, Georgeanne, 1943– Aperitif:
recipes for simple pleasures in the French Style / by Georgeanne
Brennan; photographs by Kathryn Kleinman. p. cm. Includes
bibliographical references and index. ISBN 0-8118-1077-1 (hc)
1. Cocktails. 2. Appetizers. 3. Cookery, French. I. Title.
TX951.B776 1997 641.8'74—dc20 96-28037 CIP
Printed in Hong Kong. Editing: Sharon
Silva. Book Design: Louise Fili.
Design Assistant:
Mary Jane
Callister.
Distributed
in Canada
by Rain-
coast Books
8680 Cambie Street
Vancouver, B.C. V6P 6M9
10 9 8 7 6 5 4 3 2 1 Chronicle Books 85 Second Street
San Francisco, CA 94105 Web Site: www.chronbooks.com

VIN DE PÊCHE

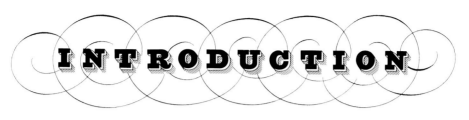

INTRODUCTION

ALTHOUGH THE RITUAL OF *L'APÉRITIF* IS COMMON THROUGHOUT THE MEDITERRANEAN REGION, IT IS IN FRANCE THAT THE TRADItion is most firmly established as a social activity enjoyed by men, women, and children, by the young and the old. Woven into the fabric of daily home life, of public and private celebrations, and of café and restaurant culture, l'apéritif is more than a drink before a meal. It is a national custom that, by deliberately setting apart time to share a drink and to socialize, engenders civility and conviviality. The beverages are rarely strong spirits and the accompanying food never satiates, as the purpose is to pique and stimulate the appetite.

In what has become an almost overwhelmingly frenzied life pace at the close of the twentieth century, *l'apéritif* has a special significance. The thirty minutes to an hour in which family, friends, acquaintances, and colleagues make a transition from the work world to the personal while sipping a beverage and nibbling a few salted nuts, all the while engaged in conversation, are welcome moments.

This book explores the French aperitif tradition, its drinks and their accompaniments. Homemade fortified wines infused and flavored with fruits, herbs, and spices are discussed and recipes provided, and the origins, history, and composition of classic aperitif drinks such as Pernod, Lillet, vermouth, and pastis are presented. Brief descriptions of some wines, both still and sparkling, typically served as aperitifs are included, as are recipes and combinations for popular nonalcoholic fruit-based aperitifs. Where pertinent, I recommend a glass of particular size or shape for serving a specific aperitif, but increasingly I find among French friends an inclination to use glasses, either old or new, that strike their fancy as well as suit the occasion.

A final chapter containing recipes for foods to serve at aperitif time covers a range of offerings, from the simplest olives and nuts to elaborate puff pastries and savory tarts. Although food-and-beverage combinations are suggested throughout the book, these are not meant to be exclusive, but simply possible pairings based on the recipes that appear in these pages.

SPARKLING WINE

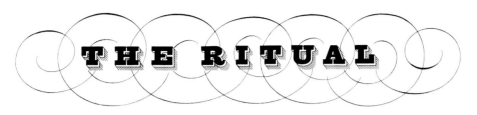

THE RITUAL

L'*APÉRITIF* IS BOTH A BEVERAGE AND A SOCIAL ACTIVITY. FIRMLY EMBEDDED IN THE FRENCH WAY OF LIFE, THIS VENERABLE CUSTOM is not exclusive to one group or another, but encompasses the whole range of the society, from stonemasons to engineers, from aristocrats to shepherds. At home, sitting around the kitchen table or gathered in the living room, outside beneath the shade of spreading trees, on terraces or balconies, family and friends come together to share an aperitif and conversation before the lunch or dinner hour. At cafés and restaurants the same ritual occurs. In twos and threes, and in groups, people meet for an aperitif. Just as the conversation and conviviality of the moment are destined to stimulate the mind and spirit, the drink serves to pique the appetite and the taste buds before the meal.

The time frame and occasion of the aperitif in France are understood. To be invited to one's home, or to invite someone to your home, for an aperitif is to agree tacitly to an interlude of half an hour to an hour of conversation, a drink, perhaps two, and a nibble of something, generally salty. After the accepted interval has elapsed, guests excuse themselves. An invitation to an aperitif does not imply that a meal will follow, or that the meeting will continue for so long that a meal becomes inevitable. Nor does an invitation mean that one can anticipate hors d'oeuvres substantial enough to comprise a meal. Instead, the aperitif is its own social occasion, complete within itself.

Meeting at a café for an aperitif follows the same convention, with neither the expectation nor obligation of a meal to follow. Of course, as with any common practice, the ritual may be altered. Many a time I have started off meeting friends for an aperitif at a café, found the conversation so agreeable, the encounter so pleasant, that by mutual consent we continued on to lunch or dinner.

I find the French aperitif a singular, quite orderly social occasion. It eliminates the uncertainty of whether or not an invitation for drinks will extend unintentionally to a greater, unplanned time commitment. Indeed, its distinct parameters encourage the extending and accepting of invitations to have a drink, as everyone understands that these are casual, relatively brief social encounters.

The ritual is aptly illustrated in the towns and villages of southern France, where by late May the café tables have been placed on the sidewalks and the trees bordering the streets and squares have leafed out, but the droves of summer tourists have yet to arrive. From noon until twelve-thirty, the café waiters are busily carrying trays held high and loaded with carafes of water for *pastis* or *citron pressé*, little bottles of Orangina, heavy-bottomed glasses filled with bright green *menthe à l'eau*, and slender-stemmed glasses of white wine. For half an hour, the cafés are alive with dust-covered cement workers, dapperly dressed sales representatives, shopkeepers, the old, the young, the middle-aged, all leaning toward one another, hands gesticulating, heads bobbing and nodding, intensely involved. By twelve-thirty the crowd has thinned, and by one o'clock only a few tables are occupied. The aperitif is over. The tables will remain sparsely populated until people begin to drift in for an after-lunch coffee before returning to work. Between seven and seven-thirty in the evening, the same phenomenon occurs. In full summer, though, when the tourists have arrived from all over Europe, and it seems as if the whole of France is on vacation along with them, the aperitif time starts later and lasts longer, and while more people are dressed in shorts than not, the ritual remains the same.

In a restaurant, however, it is already determined that one is having a meal, and the aperitif may be taken at the table. Whether the table is cloaked with starched white linen and gleams with silver and crystal, or is covered with a sheet of rustling paper and set with stainless steel, the offer of an aperitif will be made. When it arrives, it may well be accompanied by a complimentary saucer of olives or pistachios, or at a fine restaurant by something more elegant prepared by the kitchen. This might be a small plate with toasts of foie gras garnished with Champagne grapes, or a platter with a terrine of freshly made eggplant caviar surrounded by tiny red and white radishes or cornichons.

Whether at home or in a café or restaurant, the aperitif is not exclusively an adult event. Children are included in the ritual and are offered fruit-flavored syrup mixed with water, lemonade, a glass of fruit juice, or a soda. When the nuts, olives, or other foods are passed, they are offered to the children as well. The aperitif, like the meal table, is traditionally viewed as an opportunity to socialize children rather than to exclude them.

The force of the aperitif as an inclusive custom shared by the entire social structure of the country is nowhere more evident than in public celebrations. It is still common for villages to have a public aperitif to which the entire community is invited, along with friends, relatives, and even passersby. If it is spring or summer, it will be held outside, generally in front of the *mairie*, or "city hall," which is commonly located on or near a tree-shaded square. Around eleven in the morning or six in the evening, depending upon whether the aperitif will be before lunch or dinner, several long tables covered with white paper are placed in front of the building. Next, glasses are lined up on the table and bottles are set out. Finally, small bowls or saucers of salted nuts, olives, and crackers are put on the table. At a precise time, say twelve noon, people appear, a short speech usually follows, the first drink is poured, and the socializing begins. For thirty or forty minutes, men, women, and children are all talking and mingling and then, as if hearing an internal bell, they begin placing their empty glasses on the tables and heading off to mealtime. Within minutes, the aperitif is over, the square emptied. If the occasion is in the colder season of fall and winter, the scene would be changed only in that the

tables would be in one of the community's public buildings, the school perhaps if a small village, or the *salle des fêtes*—the equivalent of a community center—if a larger village.

Aperitif receptions are commonly given to acknowledge events as diverse as the opening of a new museum or gallery exhibit or the honoring of a retiring employee. They are also expected on certain occasions. It is a tradition in Provence, for example, that once the construction on a house is finished, all of the workmen, the neighbors, and friends are invited to an aperitif to *arroser la maison,* that is, to drink to the house and celebrate the job done. Everyone involved has a chance to see the final results. The workmen are heaped with praise for their fine efforts, and the owners are congratulated by friends and neighbors on being so fortunate as to have such wonderful workers. Everyone recounts his or her before and after stories. The plumber, for example, might lead a small tour to inspect a particularly difficult pipe placement, or the mason might give a demonstration showing how he flicked his wrist in a certain way to achieve the look of the plaster near the fireplace. All in all, there is much congratulatory back patting and enthusiasms during the hour the aperitifs are drunk and the plates of food are depleted of their samplings.

Weddings and baptisms are de rigueur occasions for hosting an aperitif. They take various forms, but almost always Champagne or sparkling wine is served and small, ribbon-tied net packets of sugar-coated almonds are passed to everyone present. In small villages, the wedding aperitif is sometimes given at the local café, with virtually the entire community invited to celebrate the marriage and drink to the bride and groom before the special guests go on to a wedding lunch or dinner.

Although Champagne is the preferred aperitif for a wedding or baptism, other gatherings typically serve numerous other drinks. With changing times, *le whiskey* has become part of the aperitif pantheon, although classically the drinks are not strong spirits, as their purpose remains that of titilating the appetite without dulling it.

The traditional aperitif drinks are varied, but may be loosely categorized in three groups. The wine group includes still and sparkling wines, fortified wines, and wine-based mixtures. A second group consists of herb- and spice-based alcohols—*pastis* and Campari, for example—that are customarily diluted with water. The third classification is fruit based and may or may not contain alcohol.

In the nineteenth century and well into the twentieth, cookbooks and household manuals included

instructions for making a variety of fortified wines—*les vins maison*—which were then served throughout the year. The recipes always start with wine, red, white, or rosé, which is then infused over a period of time with fruit leaves, green or ripe fruits, flowers, herbs, or spices. *Vin de noix*, for example, derives its particular flavor from green walnuts. Sugar and eau-de-vie, the brandy made from the distillation of the skins and stems that remain after wine pressing, are added to fortify and preserve the aperitif wine before bottling and corking it.

The first time I was offered a glass of a *vin maison* was by neighbors of short acquaintance in Provence who invited me and my husband and daughter to their house for an aperitif before lunch. When we arrived, a small, round outdoor table had already been set with a tray of several bottles, five glasses, a little bowl of ice cubes, a carafe of water, and a dish of tiny olives. After inviting us to sit down and exchanging pleasantries, M. Brumaire explained that he had brought out a *vin de noix* that he himself had made five years earlier, and that he thought would be nicely aged. He continued, saying that although we might prefer a *pastis*, Dubonnet, or orange juice, indicating the other bottles on the tray, he really would like us to sample his *vin de noix*.

My husband and I both accepted. M. Brumaire carefully poured about an inch and a half of the very dark brown liquid into a small, heavy-bottomed glass and handed it to me. He poured another for my husband, one for Mme Brumaire, and one for himself, and then ceremoniously offered our four-year-old daughter a small glass of orange juice, to which she assented. He asked her if she would like the juice with or without ice cubes. She chose with, and the glass was poured and handed to her. Monsieur raised his glass, said *"salut,"* we replied *"salut,"* and all took a sip. The taste of the *vin de noix* was sweet at first, followed with a spicy, slightly tart finish. It was very, very good.

Many people in France continue to make *vin de noix*, *vin d'orange,* and other fortified wines at home. They are also being made commercially now, by small-scale artisanal producers. Once considered out of style, they are back in fashion to such an extent that some restaurants, both in France and in the United States, make and serve their own *vins maison.*

Because other fortified wines are more complex and more demanding to create than the *vins maison*, they are manufactured commercially by experts using traditions of long-standing, with methods and formulas that have been carefully guarded and passed down through the years. The most popular of these wines include sherry, sweet vermouth, dry vermouth, and the regional specialties, Lillet and Pineau des Charentes.

Wines of all kinds are used in France on their own as aperitifs, and each region has its specialties. The areas of Tavel and Bandol in Provence produce highly regarded rosé wines, a common aperitif in the south, while in the area of Angers, near the egress of the Loire River, one is more likely to be offered a glass of crisp, white Muscadet, and in the Alpine region of Savoy, a sparkling *vin de Bougy.* In the great wine production regions of Burgundy, Bordeaux, Alsace-Lorraine, and the Rhône Valley, the possibilities are myriad.

Champagne and sparkling wine made by the *méthode champenoise* are served throughout France as aperitifs, and special drinks are made by adding a little liqueur to the Champagne, or to a wine. *Crème de cassis,* for example, may be added to Champagne to create *kir royale,* to white wine to make a *kir,* and to red wine for a *camisard. Vins doux naturels,* sweet fortified wines such as Beaumes-de-Venise or Banyuls, are served, as are other sweet wines, including Sauternes and Jurançon.

Pastis and Campari are two of the best-known herb- and spice-infused alcoholic aperitifs. The actual ingredients and their proportions are kept secret by the manufacturers, but the taste of *pastis* is dominated by the licorice-flavored *anis.* The less well-known Suze, Aveze, and Salers are based on the root of the yellow gentian, which gives them their characteristic bitter taste, while L'Amer Picon is flavored with quinine bark and bitter orange.

An aperitif, though, need not be alcoholic. It is the conviviality and conversation, the social inter-action, that is most important. Thus the drink might well be a glass of lemonade or grape or tomato juice. Of sustained popularity are concentrated fruit- and nut-flavored syrups, plus mint, to which water or lemonade are added.

Because the aperitif by definition is a prelude to a meal, the accompaniments, like the drinks, are tantalizers to the taste buds, enlivening them for the lunch or dinner to come. Generally, the accompaniments are bite-sized finger foods that can be eaten out of hand. Salty foods are popular—chips, olives, nuts—and these can be purchased or homemade. Salty cheeses, such as Parmesan, especially in combination with something sweet like dates or dried figs, make good accompaniments to sherry, a sweet muscat wine, or other rich drinks. Spreads made from olives, anchovies, or salt cod and served on toasts or tucked into puff pastries are common fare and, like olives, nuts, and chips, go well with virtually everything from Champagne to Suze. An elaborate occasion might bring forth truffled puff pastries, a plate of risotto croquettes. A more casual one would more likely produce a platter of tiny clams or mussels to be eaten one by one, with licking of fingers after each discarded shell. Wine bars have blackboards listing suggestions to accompany *l'apero* such as *saucisson*, which comes on a small cutting board with a sharp knife for slicing and a basket of bread alongside, or *apero*-sized goat cheeses marinated in herbed olive oil.

Although the notion of the aperitif and the beverages themselves are not exclusive to France, it is there where the ritual is part of the patrimony for women and children, as well as for men, for people of all ages, and in all stations of life. It is in France, too, that the aperitif, no matter how enjoyable, no matter how exhilarating the conversation, remains the brief, defined encounter that precedes the main event, the meal. The latter might consist of only a bowl of thick soup, or it might be several courses, but in either instance, the appetite is piqued, and the mind and the palate are prepared for the repast that lies ahead.

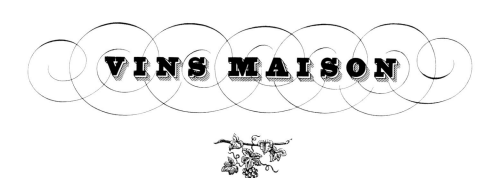

VINS MAISON

APERITIF WINES MADE AT HOME SPEAK OF AN ALCHEMY OF HIS-
TORY, PLEASURE, AND NATURE. THE NOTION OF CREATING AND BOT-
tling special wines to be stored away and brought out only at certain
times is to participate in a tradition that goes back centuries to
stone castles and farmhouses illuminated by chimney light and
candles. To pick up a bottle dark with *vin de noix,* the oil of the walnuts leaving a slight
film on its inner neck, and to remove first the sealing wax and then the cork before finally
pouring a glass of wine for a guest—or yourself—is a most satisfactory feeling. With the
first sip comes the memory of gathering the walnuts, picking them green when the trees

were still bright with spring's flush. The choosing of the wine to use, the steeping and the filtering, sugaring and tasting, pouring, then sealing, all is done over time with the anticipation of a taste to be savored months later.

Vins maison have a seasonal rhythm. Today, as in the past, the collection of the flavorings as they ripen with the seasons and the preparation of homemade aperitifs are a part of the ritual of French country life. In spring, some of the first young peach and cherry leaves are amassed to make *vin de pêche* and *guignolet;* later, ripe cherries compose the flavoring agent, while summer herbs and winter oranges yield other seasonal flavors. Fall grapes are crushed to make the *vin cuit,* a traditional Christmas drink.

These homemade aperitif wines are easy to make because generally they require only the assemblage of measured ingredients, not the skill and scientific training of a wine maker. The novice, even in the smallest of home kitchens, can transform a few bottles of red wine into *vin de cerise, guignolet, vin d'orange,* or *vin marquis* by adding flavoring agents—fruits, leaves, herbs, spices—sugar, and spirits. The end result is sweet because of the sugar and higher in alcohol content than wine because of the spirits—the fortification—which make the wines both too sweet and too potent to drink throughout a meal or for casual quaffing.

The wines traditionally used for making these beverages are the simple, straightforward, everyday table wines of any given region in France. A fine wine, one full of the balanced complexities of vine, climate, earth, and aging, should be savored on its own. In France, I can do as the French do and make *vins maison* with inexpensive young wine purchased in bulk from local wine cooperatives or producers. This is easily done by bringing reusable plastic jugs or wicker-wrapped glass vessels called *bonbonnes* in ten- and twenty-liter sizes to the winery, where they are quickly filled with the hoses attached to the huge vats.

At home in California, I purchase inexpensive domestic Pinot Noir, Merlot, Gamay, and Zinfandel for red wine–based *vins maison,* and Sauvignon Blanc, Chenin Blanc, or Sémillon for those based on white wines—or I purchase imported wines made from the same or similar grape varieties or blends. For a *vin maison* based on a rosé wine, I substitute white wine because the majority of American-made rosé wines are considerably sweeter than the French-style rosés, and do not make a comparable aperitif.

Although your choice should be neither a great nor an expensive wine, it should be of a quality you would drink, just as you would use a drinkable wine for cooking. A bad wine cannot be permutated into a good *vin maison*.

In the past, the fortification spirit most frequently used for *vins maison* was an eau-de-vie or an eau-de-vie de marc, an alcohol distilled from mediocre wine or from the residue left after the fermentation of grapes in the wine-making process. Distillation was a part of farmstead life. Today, however, grain alcohol at 90 proof or vodka at 45 proof are suitable because they are less expensive than the commercially available eau-de-vie and marc and have a neutral taste, which is desirable. In the United States, vodka and grain alcohol (Everclear is a popular brand) are both readily available, and the higher the proof, the less is required to fortify the wines to 16 degrees, the amount necessary to preserve the wine and to prevent spoilage.

For bottling *vins maison*, recycled wine bottles, cleaned and sterilized, are ideal, or new bottles may be purchased from a wine-making supply store. (See page 138 for mail-order sources.) New corks, however, not recycled ones, should be used to avoid the possibility of off flavors. The corks are dipped into boiling water to sterilize and soften them so they are malleable enough to compress and fit snugly into the bottle neck. A final step, more for effect than necessity, is to seal the corks with sealing wax,

which can also be purchased from a wine-making supply store.

Once bottled and corked, fortified *vins maison* should be labeled with date and contents and then stored in a cool, dark place such as a cellar or pantry. Some are best served within the year, while others improve with time and may be consumed several years hence. The ideal period is indicated in each recipe that follows.

A few of the *vins maison* included in this chapter are meant to be drunk at the moment they are made. A few others are not fortified, making them appropriate to drink both throughout the meal, and as an aperitif. They are all generally served in short-stemmed wineglasses or in heavy-bottomed bistro glasses. Fruit juice glasses, too, are suitable.

GENERAL INSTRUCTIONS FOR VINS MAISON

TO PREPARE THE CORKS

Before bottling a *vin maison*, soak the corks (remember, they should be new) in boiling water for 2 to 3 minutes to render them supple.

TO PREPARE THE BOTTLES

Using a bottle brush, thoroughly wash the bottles with hot, soapy water. If they still have labels and they do not slip off in the hot water, consider using rubbing alcohol or a similar product to dissolve the glue attaching them. Rinse thoroughly in clean hot water to remove any trace of soap. Place the bottles in a large kettle and add water to cover by 3 inches. Bring the water to a boil and boil for 10 minutes to sterilize thoroughly. Remove with tongs and place upside down on a rack to dry.

TO CORK THE BOTTLES

A manual corking machine, purchased at a wine-making supply store, is useful if you are doing more than a few bottles of *vin maison*. It forces the cork completely inside the neck of the bottle, which is nigh impossible to do by brute force. Use the corker according to the manufacturer's instructions.

Alternatively, place the smallest end of the cork in the bottle and push as hard as you can. Do not be deterred by a cork that sticks above the surface of the rim, however. On many occasions, I have seen French neighbors prepare a bottle or two of different *vins maison*, and cork them by hand, not bothering to bring out the corking machine; months later, I have sampled the delicious result.

TO SEAL CORKED BOTTLES

Although not necessary, sealing wax, sold in wine-supply stores, is an attractive way to protect the wine further. There are two kinds, chip wax and no chip wax. Both come in a variety of colors, including silver and gold. Chip wax comes in ½-pound cakes; the no chip comes in ¼-pound cakes. The chip wax is generally imported from France, while the no chip is made domestically. The no chip wax is easier to use, and can be applied to bottles that have been sealed by hand, a method that seldom results in a cork level with the rim. Chip wax should be used only on bottles in which the cork and the neck form an even surface. The following methods for using the two types of wax each results in enough wax to seal about twenty 750-milliliter wine bottles.

TO SEAL WITH NO CHIP WAX

The bottles should be at room temperature. In a saucepan or electric fryer restricted to this use, heat 2 cakes (¼ pound each) wax to 375 to 380 degrees F. Use an instant-read or standard thermometer to test the temperature if in a saucepan; in an electric fryer, set the temperature control.

Once the wax has reached the appropriate temperature, dip a bottle neck into the wax so that the cork is fully obscured, then take the bottle out. Still holding the bottle neck down, let the wax drip for 3 or 4 seconds, then turn the bottle upright and let stand on a countertop or table to cool and harden.

If you don't use all the wax, let it cool completely, cover the pan, and store it until you need it again.

When you are ready to uncork the bottle, cut into the wax with the short blade on a wine opener and peel it away.

TO SEAL WITH CHIP WAX

The bottles should be at room temperature and the corks dry and level with the bottle rims. It is best to use a double boiler to melt the wax, as it will have flammable paraffin added to it and the double boiler keeps the paraffin away from direct heat. Place 1 cake (½ pound) chip wax in the top pan of the double boiler over gently simmering water. The wax should be melted slowly and stirred as it melts with a wooden spoon. Add ½ to 1 ounce paraffin to the melting wax, which will help to homogenize the wax and to diminish bubbling and cracking as the wax hardens on the bottles. When the wax has become molten, test the temperature with an instant-read or standard thermometer. An ideal temperature is between 100 and 110 degrees F for colors, but gold or silver wax requires a higher temperature of 130 to 140 degrees F.

Coat the neck of each bottle with the wax as described for no chip wax, and then store any leftover wax as directed as well.

When you are ready to uncork the bottle, tap into the wax seal with the short blade on a wine opener and chip away the wax. Do not do this at the table, as it is quite messy.

VIN DE NOIX

*V*IN DE NOIX IS A FAVORITE HOMEMADE APERITIF IN AREAS OF FRANCE AND ITALY WHERE WALNUT TREES ARE COMMONLY FOUND. NOT SURPRISINGLY, RECIPES VARY FROM FAMILY TO family and region to region.

Passed down from generation to generation are such directives as that the walnuts used to flavor the wine are best harvested on the first day of summer, or on the feast day of Saint Jean, June 24, although the "season" of green walnuts is considered to last until the feast day of Sainte Madeleine, July 22. The principle is that the walnuts must be immature, and the shell not yet formed beneath the thick green skin. The developing walnuts must be still tender enough to be pierced through with a needle.

But in northern California, where I live, the walnuts have already begun to harden by the third week in June, and are solid by late July! I find that I must harvest them between late May and mid-June. I use the varieties that grow nearby, but any may be used.

Vin de noix is one of the aperitif wines that improves with age, and though, understandably, sampling must be done at the moment of bottling, one should wait at least three months, preferably six, or even a year before serving it. Initially, the taste will be quite sweet, with a burst of walnut on the finish, but with time, the sweetness and the walnut blend to a delectable spiciness. It may be served with salty appetizers: olives, of course, chips, toasted nuts. I like it especially with toasts, spread with a little fresh goat cheese or with a lightly spiced red pepper spread (page 108).

VIN DE NOIX I
From M. Albert of Moustiers Ste.-Marie, a mountain village in Haute-Provence.

With a wooden mallet or a wooden spoon, strike the walnuts just hard enough to crack open the green outer covering. Put them in a clean, dry widemouthed glass jar or ceramic crock large enough to hold them and the wine. Pour in the wine. Cover the jar or crock, put it in a cool, dark place, and let stand for 40 days. At the end of that time, using a fine-mesh sieve lined with several layers of cheesecloth, strain the wine into a clean, dry crock, jar, or any nonreactive pot large enough to hold it. (I use an enameled jam-making kettle.) Discard the walnuts.

Prepare corks and bottles as directed on page 27.

35 green walnuts

*6⅔ bottles (750 ml each)
dry red wine such as
Zinfandel, Merlot, Pinot
Noir, or Burgundy*

1 quart vodka

*2¼ pounds (4½ cups)
granulated sugar*

Pour the vodka into a nonreactive pot or bowl. Add the sugar and stir until it has dissolved, about 10 minutes. Pour the sugar-vodka mixture into the wine and stir well. Using a funnel and a ladle, fill the bottles with the now-fortified wine to within 1½ to 2 inches of the tops. Cork and seal the bottles as directed on pages 27–29.

Label and date the bottles, then store them in a cool, dark place, where they may be kept for several years. M. Abert recommends waiting for at least a year before serving the *vin de noix*. Once opened, store, tightly corked, in the refrigerator or in a cool, dark place, where it will keep up to a year. Serve at cool room temperature, pouring 2 to 3 ounces into each glass.

MAKES APPROXIMATELY EIGHT 750-ML BOTTLES

VIN DE NOIX II
In the style of Mme Marcelle Fine of Sisteron in Haute-Provence.

With a wooden mallet or spoon, strike the walnuts just hard enough to crack the green outer coverings. Combine all the ingredients in a clean, dry widemouthed glass jar or ceramic crock large enough to hold them. Cover the jar, put it in a cool, dark place, and let stand for 50 days. Then, using a fine-mesh sieve lined with several layers of cheesecloth, strain the wine into a clean, dry crock, jar, or any nonreactive pot large enough to hold it. Discard the walnuts and the vanilla bean.

30 to 35 green walnuts

*6⅔ bottles (750 ml each)
dry red wine such as
Zinfandel, Merlot, Pinot
Noir, or Burgundy*

*2¼ pounds (4½ cups)
granulated sugar*

*1 vanilla bean, approximately
10 inches long*

1 quart vodka

Prepare the corks and bottles as directed on page 27. Using a funnel and a ladle, fill the bottles with the wine to within 1½ to 2 inches of the tops. Cork and seal the bottles as directed on pages 27–29.

Label, date, then store the bottles in a cool, dark place for up to several years. Mme Fine recommends waiting at least 3 months before serving the *vin de noix*. Once opened, store, tightly corked, in the refrigerator or in a cool, dark place, where it will keep up to a year. Serve at cool room temperature, pouring 2 to 3 ounces into each glass.

MAKES APPROXIMATELY EIGHT 750-ML BOTTLES

VIN D'ORANGE

I LOVE THIS APERITIF IN SUMMERTIME. IT TASTES RICH AND DEEP, SPICED WITH THE UNDER-LYING BITE OF THE PEEL OF BITTER ORANGE—LONG SINCE REMOVED—THAT WAS USED TO infuse the wine with its distinctive flavor. Different recipes call for different wines. I generally make the red-wine version because good red wine is readily available to me, while a dry, French-style rosé is not. California rosé wines are much sweeter than French ones, and when used as the base for *vin d'orange*, they do not produce the same result. My friend Pascal uses a dry, fruity rosé wine from Bandol in the department of the Var, where he lives. He buys the wine in bulk, and then makes twenty or thirty bottles just before Christmas, using the seasonal bitter oranges that come to the markets from Spain and Algeria. By the end of March, the *vin d'orange* is ready to drink and by the end of August, once all the summer's visitors are gone, so, too, is the *vin d'orange*.

Georgina Fine taught me how to make a *vin d'orange* that she calls the poor man's version. During World War II, when she was a child, peels of oranges—any kind—were saved and hung to dry in the kitchen rafters. When there were enough, the wine was made. Buying bitter oranges, the preferred variety, only to flavor an aperitif rather than to eat seemed too great a luxury in those days.

A chilled glass of *vin d'orange* might be accompanied with *tapenade* (page 106) or anchovy toasts (page 131) or a plate of tiny stuffed tomatoes (page 118), as well as such simpler fare as nuts and olives.

❈

TRADITIONAL VIN D'ORANGE

6 ⅔ bottles (750 ml each) French-style rosé or dry white wine such as Sauvignon Blanc or Sémillon

½ quart vodka

1 pound (2 cups) granulated sugar

2 vanilla beans, each approximately 10 inches long

1 lemon, cut into several pieces

peels from 6 Seville or other bitter oranges

Combine all the ingredients in a clean, dry widemouthed glass jar or ceramic crock. Cover and store in a cool, dark place for 1 month, turning it upside down or stirring it each day for 1 week, or until the sugar has dissolved. At the end of the month, using a fine-mesh sieve lined with several layers of cheesecloth, strain the wine into a clean, dry crock, jar, or any nonreactive pot. Discard the peels, lemon, and vanilla beans.

Prepare the corks and bottles as directed on page 27. Using a funnel and a ladle, fill the bottles with the now-fortified wine to

within 1½ to 2 inches of the tops. Cork and seal the bottles as directed on pages 27–29.

Label and date the bottles, then store them in a cool, dark place, where they will keep for up to a year. The wine is ready to drink in 2 months. Once opened, store, tightly corked, in the refrigerator or in a cool, dark place, where it will keep for several months.

Serve slightly chilled or with ice cubes, pouring 2 to 3 ounces into each glass.

MAKES APPROXIMATELY SEVEN 750-ML BOTTLES

POOR MAN'S VIN D'ORANGE

A day or two before making the wine, remove the peels from the oranges and place them on a baking sheet in a 200 degree F oven for 45 minutes to dry them.

Combine all the ingredients in a clean, dry widemouthed glass jar or ceramic crock. Cover and store in a cool, dark place, turning it upside down several times each day for 1 week, or until the sugar has dissolved. Then let stand for a least 1 month but preferably for 2 or 3 months. At the end of this time, using a fine-mesh sieve lined with several layers of cheesecloth, strain the wine into a clean, dry crock, jar, or any non-reactive pot. Discard the peels.

1 bottle (750 ml) dry red wine such as Zinfandel, Merlot, Pinot Noir, Gamay, or Burgundy

¾ cup granulated sugar

½ cup vodka

dried peels from 6 small or 4 large sweet oranges (see note)

Prepare a cork and a wine bottle as directed on page 27. Using a funnel and a ladle, fill the bottle with the now-fortified wine to within 1½ to 2 inches of the top. Cork and seal as directed on pages 27–29.

Label and date the bottle, then store it in a cool, dark place. The wine is ready to drink once it has been bottled, but the flavor will improve if it is left to stand for another 2 or 3 months. The wine will keep, unopened, for up to a year. Once opened, store, tightly corked, in the refrigerator or in a cool, dark place, where it will keep for several months.

Serve slightly chilled or with ice cubes, pouring 2 to 3 ounces into each glass.

MAKES ONE 750-ML BOTTLE

VIN DE PÊCHE

WO *VINS DE PÊCHE* FOLLOW. THE FIRST IS NEITHER SUGARED NOR FORTIFIED; IT IS SIMPLY A MELLOW, FRUITY WHITE WINE INFUSED WITH PEACH LEAVES AND BLOSSOMS, CINNAMON stick, and vanilla bean. It goes well with the simplest of appetizers—a plate of young radishes (page 102) or peas in the pod (page 102)—or with more elaborate savories such as an onion tart (page 114). The second is also made with peach leaves, but it is fortified, producing an aperitif that has a slightly resinous, yet full, ripe peach flavor. Rosemary-walnut *biscotti* (page 117), toasts spread with onion *confit* (page 129) or a fresh goat cheese will underscore the aperitif's flavor.

SIMPLE VIN DE PÊCHE

Combine all the ingredients in a clean, dry widemouthed glass jar or ceramic crock. Cover and store in a cool, dark place for 10 days. At the end of that time, using a fine-mesh sieve lined with several layers of cheesecloth, strain the wine, into a clean, dry crock, jar or any nonreactive pot. Discard the leaves (and blossoms), cinnamon, and vanilla bean.

1¾ cups peach leaves and blossoms, or young (before fruit is ripe) leaves only, carefully rinsed and dried

1 bottle (750 ml) medium-dry white wine such as Chenin Blanc, Riesling, or Gewürztraminer

1 cinnamon stick, approximately 2 inches long

1 piece vanilla bean, approximately 2 inches long

Prepare a cork and wine bottle as directed on page 27. Using a funnel and a ladle, fill the bottle with the wine to within 1½ to 2 inches of the top. Cork as directed on page 27, but since this is not a wine to store over time, there is no need to seal it with wax.

Label and date the bottle, then store in the refrigerator. Drink within the month. Serve slightly chilled or with ice cubes, pouring 3 to 4 ounces into each glass.

MAKES ONE 750-ML BOTTLE

Combine all the ingredients in a clean, dry widemouthed glass jar or ceramic crock. Cover and store in a cool, dark place for 45 days, stirring every day for the first week to 10 days, or until the sugar has fully dissolved. At the end of 45 days, using a fine-mesh sieve lined with several layers of cheesecloth, strain the wine into a clean, dry crock, jar, or any nonreactive pot. Discard the leaves.

6 cups young peach leaves, picked in early summer before any fruit has developed on the tree, carefully rinsed and dried

5 bottles (750 ml each) dry white wine such as Sauvignon Blanc or Sémillon or a French-style rosé

½ quart vodka

1 pound (2 cups) granulated sugar

Prepare the corks and wine bottles as directed on page 27. Using a funnel and a ladle, fill the bottles with the now-fortified wine to within 1½ to 2 inches of the tops. Cork and seal the bottles as directed on pages 27–29.

Label and date the bottles, then store them in a cool, dark place. The wine is ready to drink now, and will keep, unopened, for up to 1 year. Once opened, store, tightly corked, in the refrigerator or in a cool, dark place, where it will keep for several months.

Serve slightly chilled or with ice cubes, pouring 2 to 3 ounces into each glass.

MAKES APPROXIMATELY SIX 750-ML BOTTLES

VIN DE GENTIANE

THE DRIED ROOTS OF THE YELLOW-FLOWERED GENTIAN (GENTIANA LUTEA) PROVIDE THE CHARACTERISTIC WILD AND BITTER BACKGROUND TASTE TO THIS SWEETENED WHITE WINE, and give it its yellow color that recalls the plant's blooms. Twenty years is considered to be the minimal time needed for the gentian plant to develop roots of adequate size and substance for drying. Once dried, the roots are used not only in making fortified wines at home, but also in the commercial production of Suze, a spirit-based aperitif, and other drinks.

In France, the dried roots are readily available in the open markets or in pharmacies. Here, they can be found at natural-food stores or through mail-order catalogs specializing in dried roots and herbs.

The bitter yet pleasing taste of the gentian, gentled by the wine and the other ingredients, goes especially well with the powerful character of salt-cured and olive oil–stored black olives and with appetizers prepared with anchovies. At the same time, it is not out of place served with mild flavors such as tiny favas in their pods (page 102), with salt for dipping.

Place the dried roots in a clean, dry widemouthed glass jar or ceramic crock large enough to hold all of the wine eventually. Add 1⅔ bottles of the wine, the sugar, vanilla bean, and the grain alcohol. Cover and store in a cool, dark place for 1 month, stirring every day for the first week, or until the sugar has fully dissolved. At the end of the month, add the remaining 5 bottles of wine and then, using a fine-mesh sieve lined with several layers of cheesecloth, strain the mixture into a clean, dry jar or crock. Discard the roots and the vanilla bean. Cover and store in a cool, dark place for 1 month longer.

1 ounce dried gentian roots

6⅔ bottles (750 ml each) medium-dry white wine such as Chenin Blanc, Riesling, or Gewürztraminer

1¾ pounds (3½ cups) granulated sugar

1 vanilla bean, approximately 10 inches long

1 cup and 2 tablespoons grain alcohol

Prepare the corks and bottles as directed on page 27. Using a funnel and a ladle, fill the bottles with the now-fortified wine to within 1½ to 2 inches of the tops. Cork and seal the bottles as directed on pages 27–29.

Label and date the bottles, then store them in a cool, dark place. The wine is ready to drink now and will keep, unopened, for up to 1 year. Once opened, store, tightly corked, in the refrigerator or in a cool, dark place, where it will keep for several months.

Serve chilled or slightly chilled, pouring 2 to 3 ounces into each glass.

MAKES APPROXIMATELY SEVEN 750-ML BOTTLES

GUIGNOLET

GUIGNOLET IS A CHERRY-FLAVORED APERITIF TRADITIONALLY MADE WITH THE SOUR CHERRIES OR LEAVES FROM TREES THAT GROW WILD IN THE MOUNTAINOUS REGIONS OF PROVENCE and in the Alps of the Savoy region. Two traditional *guignolets* are given here, one using both ripe sour cherries and cherry leaves, and one using only the leaves. A nontraditional *guignolet* that calls for sweet cherries rather than sour follows them. The three approaches, which utilize what is at

hand, epitomize for me the seasonality and adaptability that dominates the making of *vins maison.*

These *vins maison* recipes come from the family collection of Georgina Fine, a native of Savoy. A salty cheese and grilled dried figs with bacon (page 107) are excellent with *guignolet.*

GUIGNOLET I

This is to be made in summer, as it requires both leaves and cherries. Because sour cherries are used, the tartness is more pronounced than that of a *guignolet* made with sweet cherries or their leaves.

60 leaves from a sour cherry tree such as Montmorency or Morello, rinsed and dried

10 sour cherries, with pits intact

¾ cup vodka

1 bottle (750 ml) dry red wine such as Zinfandel, Merlot, Pinot Noir, or Burgundy

⅓ cup granulated sugar

Put the leaves, cherries, vodka, red wine, and sugar in a clean, dry widemouthed glass jar or ceramic crock. Cover and let stand in a cool, dark place for 15 days. At the end of that time, using a fine-mesh sieve lined with several layers of cheesecloth, strain the wine into a clean jar, crock, or any nonreactive pot. Discard the leaves; reserve the cherries, if desired, for spooning over ice cream or cake.

Prepare a cork and a bottle as directed on page 27. Using a funnel and a ladle, fill the bottle with the wine to within 1½ to 2 inches of the top. Cork and seal the bottle as directed on pages 27–29.

Label and date the bottle, then store in a cool, dark place. The wine is ready to drink now, but it will keep for up to 1 year. Once opened, store, tightly corked, in the refrigerator or in a cool, dark place, where it will keep for several months.

Served slightly chilled or at cool room temperature, pouring 2 to 3 ounces in each glass.

MAKES ONE 750-ML BOTTLE

GUIGNOLET II

In fall, when the leaves are still green on the cherry tree, they are collected and the wine is infused. According to tradition, the harvest takes place around October 22, and after fifty-eight days—around December 20—the wine is ready, just in time for Christmas. The leaves impart a rich, true cherry taste to the red wine, yet the final flavor is distinctly spicy.

Combine the leaves and the red wine in a clean, dry widemouthed glass jar or ceramic crock.

55 leaves from a sweet cherry tree, carefully rinsed and dried

1 bottle (750 ml) dry red wine such as Zinfandel, Merlot, Pinot Noir, or Burgundy

½ cup granulated sugar

⅓ cup vodka

1 piece vanilla bean, approximately 2 inches long

Cover and store in a cool, dark place for 10 days. Then, using a fine-mesh sieve lined with several layers of cheesecloth, strain the wine into a clean, dry jar or crock. Discard the leaves. Add the sugar, vodka, and vanilla and stir until the sugar has dissolved. Cover and store in a cool, dark place for 48 days. At the end of that time, strain the wine again through a cheesecloth-lined sieve into a jar, crock, or any nonreactive pot.

Prepare a cork and bottle as directed on page 27. Using a funnel and ladle, fill the bottle with the now-fortified wine to within 1½ to 2 inches of the top. Cork and seal as directed on pages 27–29.

Label and date the bottle, then store in a cool, dark place. The wine is ready to drink now, but it will keep for up to 1 year. Once opened, store, tightly corked, in a cool, dark place or in the refrigerator, where it will keep for several months.

Serve slightly chilled or at cool room temperature, pouring 2 to 3 ounces into each glass.

MAKES ONE 750-ML BOTTLE

GUIGNOLET III

The confectioners' sugar, a large amount of cherries, and the use of kirsch, a distilled cherry alcohol, as the fortifying agent make this wine intensely cherry tasting. Spicy black bean wontons (page 112), a saucer of toasted almonds, or individual-sized *gougères* (page 111) are good complements to this aperitif.

1 pound cherries, preferably sweet black such as Black Tartarian or Bing

1 bottle (750 ml) dry red wine such as Zinfandel, Merlot, Pinot Noir, or Burgundy

1½ cups confectioners' sugar

¼ cup kirsch

Use only healthy cherries, discarding any blemished ones. Remove and discard the cherry stems. Pit them by gently squeezing each fruit until the pit pops out, leaving the cherry whole. This technique works well only on fully ripe cherries, so it may be necessary to use a knife or a cherry pitter. Combine the pitted cherries, wine, and sugar in a stainless-steel or other nonreactive saucepan and place over medium-high heat. Bring the mixture to a gentle boil, stirring to dissolve the sugar. Reduce the heat to medium and

cook for 5 minutes. Remove from the heat and let cool.

Transfer the mixture to a clean, dry widemouthed glass jar or ceramic crock. Add the kirsch, cover, and let stand in a cool, dark place for 2 days. At the end of that time, using a fine-mesh sieve lined with several layers of cheesecloth, strain the wine into a clean, dry jar, crock, or any nonreactive pot. Save the cherries to use for cooking, or to spoon over ice cream or cake.

Prepare a cork and a bottle as directed on page 27. Using a funnel and a ladle, fill the bottle with the now-fortified wine to within $1\frac{1}{2}$ to 2 inches of the top. Cork and seal the bottle as directed on pages 27–29. Label and date the bottle, then store in a cool, dark place. The wine is ready to drink now, but it will keep for up to 1 year. Once opened, store, tightly corked, in a cool, dark place or in the refrigerator, where it will keep for several months.

Serve slightly chilled or at cool room temperature, pouring 2 to 3 ounces into each glass.

MAKES ONE 750-ML BOTTLE

VIN MARQUIS

RICH, MAHOGANY COLORED, SWEET, AND SMOOTH TO DRINK, *VIN MARQUIS* IS ONE OF THE HOMEMADE APERITIF WINES, LIKE *VIN DE NOIX*, THAT BENEFITS FROM AGING, ESPECIALLY IF made with a red wine. Although it can be served within six months of bottling, its deep flavor, tinged with memories of vanilla and citrus, mellows over time, and the bottles can be kept for several years.

A friend in France, Michele, upon the death of his father in 1994, cleared out the family home in Toulon, including the wine cellar. Among the dust- and cobweb-covered vintage wine bottles were a dozen of *vin marquis* made by Michele's mother in 1983, 1986, and 1987. At twelve years old, the 1983 was no longer drinkable. Several of the 1986 bottles were superb, as were all of the 1987 ones. Michele's mother, Marcelle, was noted in the extended family for her excellent *vin marquis*. The recipe that follows is based upon hers, taken from her personal *cahier des recettes*.

VIN MARQUIS À LA MARCELLE

Combine all the ingredients in a clean, dry widemouthed glass jar or ceramic crock. Cover and place in a cool, dark place for 40 days. At the end of that time, using a fine-mesh sieve lined with several

6 ⅔ bottles (750 ml each) French-style rosé, medium-dry white wine such as Chenin Blanc, Riesling, or Gewürztraminer; or a red wine such as Zinfandel, Merlot, Pinot Noir, Gamay, or Burgundy

6 or 7 sweet oranges, cut into 2-inch pieces

1 lemon, cut into 2-inch pieces

2 pounds (4 cups) plus ¼ cup granulated sugar

1 vanilla bean

3¾ cups vodka

layers of cheesecloth, strain the wine into a clean jar, crock, or any nonreactive pot. Discard the oranges, lemon, and vanilla bean.

Prepare the corks and bottles as directed on page 27. Using a funnel and a ladle, fill the bottles with the now-fortified wine to within 1½ to 2 inches of the tops. Cork and seal the bottles as described on pages 27–29.

Label and date the bottles, then store in a cool, dark place for at least 6 months before serving. The wine will keep for 3 or 4 years. Once opened, store, tightly corked, in a cool, dark place or in the refrigerator, where it will keep for up to a year.

Serve slightly chilled, pouring about 2 ounces into each glass.

MAKES APPROXIMATELY EIGHT 750-ML BOTTLES

SANGRIA

SANGRIA

SANGRIA IS TYPICALLY ASSOCIATED WITH SPAIN, WHERE IT IS ESPECIALLY POPULAR ALONG THE COAST NEAR BARCELONA. MANY VERSIONS EXIST, BUT BASICALLY SANGRIA IS A MIXTURE of red wine with citrus or other fruits, with or without the addition of sparkling water or flavored sodas. Since it is not fortified, it should be served at the time it is made, either from a punch bowl or pitcher, chilled or with ice cubes. A festive drink, it goes well with spicy, salty foods.

1 bottle (750 ml) dry red wine such as Zinfandel, Merlot, Pinot Noir, or Burgundy, chilled

2 oranges, cut crosswise into slices

2 lemons, cut crosswise into slices

1 bottle (12 ounces) sparkling mineral water, chilled

Combine all the ingredients in a punch bowl or pitcher and serve immediately.

MAKES 4 TO 6 SERVINGS

VIN CHAUD

HOT WINE, USUALLY FLAVORED WITH HERBS OR SPICES AND PERHAPS A DASH OF BRANDY, MAKES A WARMING APERITIF TO SERVE DURING THE COLD MONTHS OF FALL AND WINTER. No maceration or storage is necessary for the preparation, as the ingredients are assembled and the wine heated shortly before serving.

VIN CHAUD WITH WHITE WINE

In this *vin chaud*, a white wine is used and lemon and brandy are added. Once hot, the drink is ignited and the dancing surface of blue flames makes a festive presentation. Pastry-based appetizers such as rosemary-walnut *biscotti* (page 117), anchovy puffs (page 109), or tiny *gougères* (page 111) are pleasingly substantial counterpoints to the hot lemon-brandied wine.

1 lemon

2 whole cloves

1 bottle (750 ml) dry white wine such as Sauvignon Blanc or Sémillon

1 cup granulated sugar

¼ cup brandy

Remove the yellow zest from the lemon skin, in wide strips if possible. Stick the cloves into the zest and set aside. Remove and discard all but a thin layer of the white pith from the lemon. Cut the lemon crosswise into 6 slices each about ¼ inch thick and set these aside as well.

In a nonreactive saucepan, combine the wine, sugar, and clove-pierced zest. Place over medium heat and bring to a simmer, stirring to dissolve the sugar. When a thin layer of frothy bubbles forms on the surface, remove from the heat and discard the lemon zest and cloves.

Pour the wine into a small punch bowl. Add the brandy, pouring it carefully across the surface, and then ignite it with a long match. Let the flames die, then ladle the hot wine into heat-resistant glasses, filling each glass with 3 to 4 ounces. Garnish each glass with a thin slice of the reserved lemon.

MAKES 6 TO 8 SERVINGS

VIN CHAUD WITH RED WINE

Here, a full-bodied red wine is used, and although the wine is slightly sweetened and fruit and spices are added, no brandy is included. A day or two before making the wine, remove the peel from an orange and from a lemon and place the peels on a baking sheet in a 200 degree F oven for 45 minutes to dry them.

1 bottle (750 ml) dry red wine such as Claret or Cabernet Sauvignon

dried peel of 1 orange (see note)

dried peel of 1 lemon (see note)

1 cinnamon stick, approximately 4 inches long

4 whole cloves

1 star anise

1 piece vanilla bean, approximately 2 inches long

¼ cup granulated sugar

A soft, slightly salty cheese such as Stilton or Maytag Blue with plain crackers or some smoky toasted almonds play well with the spiciness of the rich wine. An anchovy spread (page 131) or a *tapenade* (page 106) is also a good choice.

Combine all the ingredients in a nonreactive saucepan. Place over medium heat and bring just to the edge of a boil, stirring to dissolve the sugar. Reduce the heat to low and simmer for 5 minutes.

To serve, ladle the hot wine into heat-resistant glasses.

MAKES 6 TO 8 SERVINGS

VIN CUIT

*L*ORE AND LEGEND ABOUND ABOUT HOW THIS WINE MUST BE MADE, BUT THERE IS AGREE-MENT THAT WHILE *VIN CUIT* IS TRADITIONAL TO SERVE WITH THE THIRTEEN DESSERTS OF A Provençal Christmas Eve supper, it also makes a fine aperitif.

In the old way, the first step of the process calls for cooking freshly pressed juice or must from sweet wine grapes in a cauldron over an open fire, stirring constantly and removing the developing froth, until the amount of juice is reduced nearly to half. The natural sugars in the fruits become concentrated and the juice itself develops a rich, full winelike taste that, to me, is reminiscent of port. Some practitioners demand the addition of pine nuts to the cooking juice, others that of quinces, and still others call for a few hot coals to give the finished wine a faintly caramelized character. Purists insist that the wine should be allowed to develop its flavor on its own.

In the second step, the mysteries begin. To become wine, the juice must be fermented, but all the natural yeasts have been killed during the cooking process. Some stories have the cooked wine being placed in open containers in the *cave* where the household's wine is already fermenting, so the local yeast in the air will be available to ferment the cooked juice. But would the resulting *vin cuit* be good? Some years yes, some years no. To avoid such variations in quality, some makers inoculate the juice immediately with a quantity of fermenting wine, so as not to leave the results open to chance. If a *cave* full of fermenting vats is not handy, one can purchase wine yeast for inoculating the juice.

At one time, commercially made versions of *vin cuit* were for sale throughout Provence, but this is no longer the case, so for many, *vin cuit* remains a childhood memory. Some small manufacturers are producing artisanal versions that are reputedly made in the old way.

Finally, a version of *vin cuit* that has been disparaged as "doctored grape juice," but that I find quite a respectable alternative to the interesting but more complex method described above, is simply to fortify the concentrated juice with alcohol. It is already an adventure to acquire and crush the twenty or so pounds of varietal wine grapes that it takes to make enough concentrated juice for two or three bottles of *vin cuit*. Standing over the stove, skimming the surface foam from my enameled kettle, watching over the juice to make sure it doesn't boil, makes me feel somewhat like a wine maker, even if I am making *vin cuit* the shortcut way.

Put the grapes in a large basin or tub. Take off your shoes and socks and crush the grapes with your feet—clean, of course—or, alternatively, crush the grapes with a hoe, releasing the juices. Once the grapes have been crushed, strain the juice through a fine-mesh sieve. Discard the seeds, stems, and skins. Measure the juice. Twenty pounds of grapes will yield 13 to 16 cups of juice, depending upon variety and time of harvest.

20 pounds red wine grapes, to make approximately 14 cups strained juice

1 cup vodka

Put the juice in a nonreactive kettle—I use an enamelware kettle that usually serves for jam making—and cook over very, very low heat until it has reduced by about 40 percent, removing any foam as it appears. This will take about 6 hours. Remove from the heat, cover with a cloth, and let cool. Once cool, using a fine-mesh sieve lined with several layers of cheesecloth, strain the juice into a large crock, jar, or any nonreactive pot.

Measure the juice; you should have approximately 8 cups. Add the vodka.

Prepare corks and bottles as directed on page 27. Using a funnel and a ladle, fill the bottles with the wine to within 1½ to 2 inches of the tops. Cork and seal the bottles as directed on pages 27–29.

Label and date the bottles, then store in a cool, dark place. The *vin cuit* is ready to drink now, but will keep for up to 6 months. Once opened, store, tightly corked, in a cool, dark place or in the refrigerator, where it will keep for several months. Serve slightly chilled or at room temperature, pouring 2 to 3 ounces into each glass.

MAKES APPROXIMATELY TWO-AND-ONE-HALF 750-ML BOTTLES

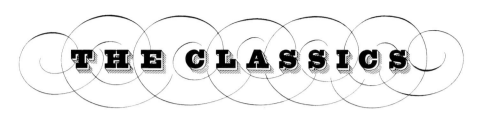

THE CLASSICS

THIS CHAPTER IS COMPRISED OF WINES, WINE-BASED APERITIFS, AND APERITIFS MADE FROM ALCOHOLS INFUSED WITH HERBS AND SPICES. The diverse group is defined by the fact that, unlike the homemade *vins maison,* which may be made successfully by any novice in a kitchen, producing fine wines and complex blends requires trained and knowledgeable people and specialized equipment for maceration, fermentation, extraction, aging, storing, and blending.

Pastis and Pernod, Suze, Campari, and L'Amer Picon are aperitifs that derive their distinctive tastes from mixtures of herbs and spices that have been steeped in alcohol.

Various filtrations and additions occur to produce the final product, the exact ingredients and proportions of which are proprietary secrets.

Imbuing alcohol with the essence of herbs and spices has a long tradition that reaches back through medieval times to the ancient civilizations of China, Egypt, Mesopotamia, Greece, and Rome. Star anise, one of the primary ingredients of today's *pastis*, was used as a flavoring agent for alcohol thousands of years ago in China. From there it made its way along the silk trade routes to the Mediterranean, where it was incorporated into infusions consumed both medicinally and for pleasure. The dried gentian root, which gives Suze its characteristic taste and color, was used in the Egypt of the pharaohs, and then later in the Middle Ages by European monks who were adept in preparing concoctions with wild and cultivated herbs.

Suze, Campari, and L'Amer Picon share the commonality of bitterness. Researchers in the science of taste tell us that bitterness is the last of the four primary tastes to be appreciated, following sugar, salt, and acid. Thus, a taste for it has become associated with sophistication and a developed palate. Campari is considered to be a drink of sophisticates throughout the Western world, but Suze, until recently, has remained a provincial specialty consumed primarily in France. Picon, flavored principally with quinine bark and bitter oranges, has not gained world fame either, although it does figure in sophisticated drinks like Picon punch.

The spirit-based aperitifs are usually combined with water and ice when served as an aperitif, but are also presented *au naturel* over ice cubes, and, in a subject not covered in this book, as important components in mixed bar drinks.

Commercially produced wine-based aperitifs fall into two main categories: those that are only wine and spirits and those that also include additional flavoring such as bitter orange, quinine, herbs, or spices. The former includes Pineau des Charentes and sherry; the latter embraces sweet and dry vermouths, whose origins can be traced to ancient Rome, and Lillet and Dubonnet, which are blends composed and commercialized in the nineteenth century.

Wine is commonly offered as an aperitif. White wines ranging from light and dry to medium and fruity to sweet are all suitable, as are the rosé wines, especially the French-style ones that are drier and more crisp than their sugary American namesakes. Red wines for aperitifs are most successfully

KIR

chosen from those that are at their peak when consumed young. Fruit liqueurs or nonalcoholic fruit syrups can also be added to white or red wines and to sparkling wines to create an aperitif.

Sparkling wine, its bubbles rising to the surface, gently popping and fizzing, is the quintessential aperitif for any festive occasion. Sparkling wines from France, Chile, Italy, Spain, Germany, the United States, and other wine-producing countries may be dry, medium dry, or sweet and pink or white, and all are suitable aperitifs, although the one most conventionally served is the driest, labeled brut. Champagne is a sparkling wine made in the Champagne region of France, and it is the only sparkling wine that may be legally labeled Champagne.

Unlike fortified aperitifs, wines, both still and sparkling, are consumed with soups, stews, salads, roasts—in short, with the whole gamut of food, including desserts. A number of sweet wines that are regularly thought of as dessert wines are also appropriate aperitifs. While some of the classic aperitif wines seem destined to be paired with rich food such as Sauternes with foie gras or Champagne with caviar or smoked salmon, none are amiss served with nuts or olives, classics themselves.

The classics comprise a wide range of different aperitifs. Some are traditionally served in a particular type of glass; for others the type of glass might depend upon whether or not ice or water or soda, for example, is added. The choice may also be determined by whether the occasion is casual or more formal. For instance, wine would be typically served in a wineglass, but for an informal gathering, a simple juice or bistro glass might be used.

In the late eighteen hundreds and early ninteen hundreds, French cafés and bistros had glasses that looked as if they would hold several ounces. In fact, they held less because the hollow part of the glass was V-shaped and rested upon a solid, substantial base. Once poured, the sweet vermouth, for example, would appear as a dark inverted cone captured in thick glass. These glasses may still be found in *brocante* and antique stores in France and are quite sought after—understandably. They are quite beautiful and it is a pleasure to feel their weight in the hand.

PASTIS

*P*ASTIS IS A GENERIC TERM FOR ANISE-FLAVORED ALCOHOL-BASED APERITIFS THAT ARE CRE-
ATED IN PART BY THE MACERATION OF HERBS AND SPICES, WITH AS MANY AS SEVENTY DIF-
ferent ones in some instances. The precise formulas, of course, are secret. Pernod is the brand
name of an anise-flavored aperitif whose manufacturing process utilizes distillation, which differen-
tiates it from *pastis*, of which there are many brands. Both of these aperitifs, however, are consumed
with water, which turns the drink cloudy.

Pastis and Pernod have a common ancestor in the fantastically popular anise-flavored absinthe of
the nineteenth century. Absinthe, which originated in the mountains of Switzerland as an herbal rem-
edy, was an alcohol-based aperitif that contained anise as well as numerous other spices and herbs, but
whose so-called degenerative powers were due to the inclusion of the herb wormwood *(Artemesia
absinthia)*. The aperitif was outlawed in France in 1915, after a national hue and cry was raised against
it as a source of moral, mental, and physical toxicity among the population. It had already been
banned in most other European countries, and in the United States in 1912. Manufacturers were
forced to close, and all alcohols containing anise became rigorously controlled by the government.
One-time producers promptly sought to create an anise-flavored drink that would capture the market
void left by absinthe, yet be acceptable to the government. Pernod Fils, the first manufacturer of
absinthe in France, had had a large popular following, and the company was able to reenter the market in 1926 with a new anise-based aperitif called simply Pernod.

Pastis is synonymous with the south of France. Flavored with star anise, green anise, fennel,
licorice roots, and various other herbs, *pastis* was first produced and popularized by Paul Ricard in
Marseilles in 1932, under his label Ricard. Boulevardiers and their ladies sipped his creation in the elegant cafés whose tables spread out onto the sidewalks of the Champs-Élysées of Marseilles, the
Canebière. At village cafés, farmers and working men asked for Ricard, and it was also served in bourgeois homes. Drawn by success, many manufacturers followed Ricard. Today, the brightly colored
umbrellas blazoned with the trade names of Ricard, "51," Berger, Casanis, and Duval bloom in the
sidewalk-café landscape of France.

The anise-flavored aperitifs have, as did absinthe, accoutrements and rituals associated with them.

Alongside the glasses, with their *dose* (portion) already poured from the bottle, stand carafes of water that resemble those of the era of absinthe. They are generally of glass or ceramic and are labeled with the manufacturer's name and logo. Special heavy-bottomed glasses are used, just as they were for absinthe. Some brands of *pastis* that do not contain sugar are sold with a filigree spoon, again reminiscent of the absinthe spoons of the last century. A sugar cube is placed in the spoon, and the *pastis* is poured over it into the glass, just as absinthe was.

Today manufacturers tout *pastis* and Pernod as low-alcohol drinks. When water is added in the recommended ratio of five to one, the alcohol content is just 6 percent, half the percentage of most wines; when mixed in the "long drink" ratio of ten to one, the alcohol content dips to but 3 percent.

Not so many years ago, home-style versions of *pastis* were made. When I first lived in Provence and discovered *pastis*, I noticed that when it was offered to me in the kitchens of local farmers or shepherds, it wasn't poured from a commercial bottle, but from old wine bottles with masking-tape labels—or no labels at all. I asked a neighbor about it, one of the farmer's wives, and she said, "Oh, we make it ourselves. It's too expensive to buy with all those government taxes." When I asked if it was legal, she said no, but everyone makes their own anyway and that I could, too. She explained that the *petit traficant*, the black marketeer, came through the area every month or so selling small vials of the secret forbidden flavorings, which were then mixed with eau-de-vie to create *pastis*. "I'll tell him to stop by your house." I was thrilled by the idea of clandestine, black-market dealings that felt dangerous and romantic.

One day, shortly after lunch, a large, old black Citroèn stopped in the middle of the road in front of my door. Behind the wheel slouched a man who could only be *le traficant*. Lighting a yellowish cigarette before getting out to open the trunk of the car and keeping the black felt hat pulled low, he mumbled to me as he lifted the lid of a small cardboard box. I kept my head down and mumbled, "I'll take two." He got the vials from the box and I surreptitiously took a hundred franc note from my pocket and gave it to him. Once inside, I examined the vials, no larger than my little finger, then hid them away, never to be used, but it was a memorable adventure.

I have been served *pastis* and Pernod in many farmhouse kitchens, but also in truck-stop restaurants, cafés, elegant dining rooms, and at weddings, receptions, and village feasts, often along with

LE PERROQUET, LA TOMATE, AND LA MAURESQUE

PASTIS, RED VERMOUTH, AND WHITE WINE

bowls of olives or pickled mushrooms or with toasts spread with onion confit (page 129) or *tapenade* (page 106). I especially enjoy it, though, at the old cafés in the small villages and out-of-the-way city neighborhoods that still have vintage peanut machines on the counter. For two francs—once only fifty centimes—you can turn the handle of the machine and fill a small saucer with salty, dry-skinned peanuts to nibble with your glass of *pastis*.

A bottle of *pastis*, once opened, can be tightly recapped and stored at room temperature for up to a year.

CLASSIC PASTIS

1 ounce pastis
5 ounces cold water
1 or 2 ice cubes (optional)

Pour the *pastis* into a glass, then the cold water. Now, add the ice cubes, if desired.

MAKES 1 SERVING

LA MAURESQUE

I was first told about the various versions of *pastis* by a neighbor in the very small village in Provence where I lived. His family had been in the region for five generations and he spoke French with a heavy accent *du midi*. He insisted I try all three versions, almond, mint, and grenadine, which he said were

1 ounce pastis
1 tablespoon almond syrup (orgeat)
5 ounces cold water
1 or 2 ice cubes (optional)

common in Provence. So, the next time I was in a large village, one with dozens of cafés, I chose a table in the sun, and when the waiter asked what I would like, I replied, *"Une mauresque, s'il vous plaît."* I was rewarded with a knowing nod, and a conversation about *pastis* and its variations, as well as the pleasure of the drink's sweet almond flavor—and a dish of small green olives. Almond syrup, sometimes labeled *orgeat,* is generally an opaque pale beige, and it seems surprising that something that looks so dull can taste so good.

Pour the *pastis* into a glass, then the almond syrup. Add the cold water, followed by the ice cubes, if desired.

MAKES 1 SERVING

◎

LA TOMATE

La tomate, not surprisingly, acquires its name from the fact that the *pastis* and water turn red when the grenadine is added. The taste, however, is not at all of tomato, but of a slightly sweetened *pastis.*

1 ounce pastis
1 tablespoon grenadine syrup
5 ounces cold water
1 or 2 ice cubes (optional)

Pour the *pastis* into a glass, then the grenadine syrup. Add the cold water, followed by the ice cubes, if desired.

MAKES 1 SERVING

◎

LE PERROQUET

Green like a parrot seen through a mist, *le perroquet* has the refreshing taste of mint.

1 ounce pastis
1 tablespoon mint syrup
5 ounces cold water
1 or 2 ice cubes (optional)

Pour the *pastis* into a glass, then the mint syrup. Add the cold water, followed by the ice cubes, if desired

MAKES 1 SERVING

RICH, SLIGHTLY FRUITY, AND SWEET, THIS DELICATE GOLD APERITIF IS MADE WITH BLENDS OF EITHER WHITE OR RED GRAPES FROM THE COGNAC-PRODUCING REGION OF CHARENTE, located north and northeast of Bordeaux. The fresh juice or must is blended with Cognac and then aged for at least a year, often longer.

Like so many of the aperitifs, Pineau des Charentes has a story of discovery that goes with it. It is said that a wine maker at a chateau mistakenly put fresh grape must in a cask that contained Cognac. He realized his mistake, but noticed that fermentation was not occurring. He put the barrel away and, in the good tradition of a legend, forgot all about it for several years. Upon its rediscovery, he saw that the color had changed to a clear gold, and that it tasted neither like Cognac nor wine, but a happy marriage of the two wrapped together by the flavor of the oak barrel, so he celebrated the discovery his error had created.

The passionate attachment the French often display to their *terroir* and its products was made tangible to me over a bottle of Pineau des Charentes. The director of a large French seed firm was hosting a lunch for me and my companion, and had invited perhaps a half-dozen colleagues. He was from Charente, and thus the aperitif offered was Pineau des Charentes, which he highly recommended, and which we accepted. The beautiful amber liquid was poured into wineglasses and handed to us. All the others but one—also from Charente—declined. Instead, each chose, and highly praised, an aperitif typical to his region: *pastis* for the plant breeder and his associate from Arles, Pernod for the Parisian, and chilled rosé wine from Chinon for the Loire Valley natives. We were served toasts with pâté de foie gras and little bowls of pistachios with our drinks.

Serve at cellar temperature or slightly chilled, pouring three to four ounces into each glass. Once opened, recork tightly and store in a cool dark place for up to two months.

*S*PARKLING WINE OR CHAMPAGNE MAKES A FINE APERITIF FOR ANY OCCASION. THE RITUAL OF UNCORKING THE BOTTLE, THE ANTICIPATION OF ITS EFFERVESCENCE, AND THE FIRST POUR-ing with bubbles ascendant are integral parts of the drink. As appropriate to precede a picnic as a wedding, dinner for two or a dozen, sparkling wines and Champagne offer a vertiginous range of tastes, and some confusion of terminology.

Sparkling wine may be flinty white and elegantly lean, or warm amber with a rich roundness that fills your mouth. It may be the color of faded roses, or palest coral, crisp, and fruity. Many are quite low in alcohol content, ranging from 6 to 8 percent, and they may be brut (the driest), dry, semidry, medium dry, or sweet.

The bubbling effect that characterizes sparkling wines of all types is triggered when carbon dioxide is released from the bottle upon opening. Most sparkling wines are made by causing the wine to undergo a second fermentation, either in individual bottles or in bulk in sealed vats. Only sparkling wine made in the Champagne region under very specific controls may legally be called Champagne, and the second fermentation in bottles is the only method allowed in the region. Here are the great Champagne houses of Veuve Cliquot, Pommery, Mumm's, Krug, Tattinger, and Moèt et Chandon. Many sparkling wines are made using the second fermentation method — *méthode champenoise* — but they may not be called Champagne.

Sparkling wines are made in the wine-producing regions of France, Italy, the United States, and Spain; in fact, they are made throughout the world. Asti, bottled in northern Italy, is one of the best known of the Italian *prosecco* wines. From a long stone's throw away, in the Savoy region of France, comes *vin de Savoie mousseux,* light and fruity, while Spain, far to the south, produces an abundance of excellent sparkling wines, as do the coastal valleys of northern California, a continent away.

Sparkling wines and Champagnes are not only superb aperitifs on their own, but they are also amenable to creative endeavors on our part. They may be flavored with a small amount of liqueur to make a whole range of aperitifs. *Crème de cassis,* the black currant liqueur that is used to create the well-known *kir royale,* is but one liqueur to consider. Chambord, a raspberry liqueur flavored with herbs and honey; Framboise de Bourgogne, made from raspberries; *liqueur de fraise* fashioned from

strawberries; and the peach-based *crème de pêche* are all good choices and each adds its particular distinction to sparkling wine. A classic combination made with freshly squeezed orange juice rather than a liqueur is the mimosa. Especially tantalizing is a mimosa made with the ruby-colored juice of blood oranges, whose berry flavor brings a surprising addition to the sparkling wine. Fine-quality fruit syrups that contain no alcohol offer a diverse sampling to combine with sparkling wines, as do puréed fruits. The Bellini, an example of the latter, calls for adding puréed white peaches to Champagne, half a peach for each glass.

For these aperitif combinations, it is not necessary to use the finest Champagne. In fact, such Champagne should be savored in its pristine state, as should the finest of the sparkling wines. Instead, one of the many inexpensive, yet good-quality domestic or imported sparkling wines can be substituted.

Glasses for drinking Champagne and sparkling wine are of many shapes and sizes. They range from shallow bowls atop short stems, which were used in the eighteenth century, to long stemmed with shallow bowls, to those most common today, the long-stemmed flute and tulip-shaped glasses that are recommended to maximize and encourage the flow of bubbles.

To open the bottle, loosen a bit of the foil to reach the wire muzzle of the cork. With a thumb on the cork, untwist the wire and remove it. With thumb and index finger of one hand firmly around the cork, turn the bottle with the other hand to loosen the cork and remove it. Be ready to pour as soon as the cork comes out.

Serve chilled, pouring three to four ounces into each glass.

FLAVORED SPARKLING WINE OR CHAMPAGNE APERITIFS

Some experts recommend putting the liqueur in the glass first and then pouring in the sparkling wine, and others insist on the reverse, sparkling wine, then the liqueur. In either case, stir to mingle the two. Each of the following combinations makes a single serving.

KIR ROYALE: ½ ounce *crème de cassis* and 4 ounces sparkling wine or Champagne.

CHAMBORD: ½ ounce Chambord and 4 ounces sparkling wine or Champagne.

FRAMBOISE: ½ ounce Framboise de Bourgogne and 4 ounces sparkling wine or Champagne.

FRAISE: ½ ounce *liqueur de fraise* and 4 ounces sparkling wine or Champagne.

PÊCHE: ½ ounce *crème de pêche* and 4 ounces sparkling wine or Champagne.

MIMOSA: The amount of sparkling wine or Champagne to freshly squeezed orange juice may be in whatever proportions preferred, generally 1 part juice (1 ounce) to 3 parts (3 ounces) wine, or equal portions of each.

WHITE WINE

WITHIN THE WHITE WINES LIE GREAT AND VARIED POSSIBILITIES FOR APERITIFS. SWEET, LATE-HARVEST WINES SUCH AS SAUTERNES, JURANÇON, AND BARSAC, MADE FROM GRAPES that have stayed long on the vine so that their sugars rise and intensify, sometimes developing botrytis, the noble rot, are as appropriate as crisp, dry wines or mellow fruity ones.

While most white wines are perfect for the aperitif enjoyed simply with olives or nuts, some truly blossom when juxtaposed with particular flavors. A bone-dry Muscadet (quite different from the similar-sounding muscat) or a Sauvignon Blanc, for example, paired with oysters straight from the shell becomes sublime, as does a viscous, full-bodied Jurançon consumed with a mousse of chicken livers spread on toasts. Mellow Gewürztraminers and fruity Rieslings seem to dance on the tongue when paired with the spicy flavors of cilantro and chilies. Hugely different from one another, yet all exemplify the purpose of an aperitif—to tantalize and stimulate the appetite.

Serve chilled, pouring three to four ounces into each glass.

KIR

The origins of *kir* may be traced to a mayor of Dijon of the same name, who purportedly combined *crème de cassis,* which is produced in the region of Dijon, with a white wine from the region of Burgundy. Typically, the wine for a *kir* should not be a fine, complex one, but rather a dry, simple white made to drink young. The dash of liqueur then heightens, not confuses the flavor of the wine.

1 tablespoon creme de cassis

4 ounces dry white wine such as Sauvignon Blanc, Grey Riesling, or Aligoté

Put the *crème de cassis* in a wineglass, pour in the white wine, and stir.

MAKES 1 SERVING

*T*HE RED WINES MOST SUITABLE FOR AN APERITIF ARE LIGHT YET FLAVORFUL, THOSE THAT ARE MEANT TO BE CONSUMED YOUNG, WITHIN TWO OR THREE YEARS OF BOTTLING, OR EVEN SOONER, as they do not carry the amount of tannin that is necessary for a wine whose destiny is to develop its flavor over time. In France, the youngest of these wines to reach the market are designated *primeur*, a term now used interchangeably with *nouveau*, and they are released in the same year the grapes were harvested. Originally, producers were permitted to release their new wines on December 15, but in the 1970s the date was changed to the third Thursday of the November following the harvest. The restriction has prompted a successful marketing strategy, and the arrival of the first wines of the new harvest is touted not just in France, but throughout Europe and North America. Cases of Beaujolais Nouveau are flown from France to arrive and be poured at nearly the same moment as the bottles are opened in France. Light and fruity, still with the taste of grape on it, and served slightly chilled, this is an ideal red aperitif wine, with a ready-made sense of festiveness.

Domestic wine makers produce Gamay (also called Gamay Beaujolais) and are beginning to emulate the French, releasing Gamay Nouveau in November. These light wines accommodate many flavors and may be served with bite-sized pizzas, onion tarts (page 114), light pastry-based appetizers, and with raw vegetables such as radishes (page 102) or peas or fava beans in the pod (page 102).

A rosé made in the French style, dry and light yet full of body and substance, is a most alluring aperitif. The taste of this chilled rose-tinted dry wine that Provence makes so well has the power to re-create the sensory experience of being there. It is amenable to small samplings of shellfish, perhaps tiny clams or mussels picked from their shells (page 125), and also forms a gustatory alliance with olives, garlic, and anchovies, the indigenous flavors of the Provence *terroir*.

A number of adventuresome California wine makers have been producing rosé wines in the drier French style from the same grape varieties used there, such as Grenache and Syrah. With names such as Angel Rosé, Vin Gris, and Vin Gris de Cigar, these are easy to identify. California's other rosé wine, White Zinfandel, often called blush because of its pale pink color, tends to be sweeter than French rosés, which come not only from Provence, but also from the Loire Valley and Savoy.

Serve young red wines at cellar temperature or slightly chilled and serve rosé wines chilled.

VINS DOUX NATURELS

THESE ARE WINES MADE FROM EITHER WHITE OR RED WINE GRAPES THAT HAVE BEEN ALLOWED TO DEVELOP A HIGH SUGAR CONTENT, THUS PRODUCING A SWEET WINE. ONCE A certain sugar percentage is reached, the fermentation is stopped by the addition of alcohol. From there, aging occurs, the length and kind depending upon the particular *vin doux* being produced. Among the best known of these are Beaumes-de-Venise, a rich golden wine made from the muscat grapes produced in vineyards of Beaumes-de-Venise in the region of the southern Rhône River, and Banyuls, which comes from southwestern France. The latter is made from Grenache grapes planted on terraces surrounding the town of Banyuls on the coast, not far from the Spanish border, where they overlook the Mediterranean Sea.

These lush, full-mouthed wines become an even richer experience when sipped with a sampling of rich foods such as foie gras or truffle slices on *tapenade* toasts, or, more simply, toasted almonds.

Serve at cool room temperature in wineglasses, pouring two to three ounces into each glass. Once opened, recork tightly and place in the refrigerator for up to two months.

SHERRY

TRUE SHERRY IS PRODUCED ONLY IN ANDALUSIA, SPAIN, ONLY IN THE REGION OF JEREZ, NOT FAR FROM THE ATLANTIC OCEAN ON SPAIN'S SOUTHERN TIP, AND IN ONLY THREE TOWNS. THEIR names sing on the tongue—Jerez de la Frontera, Puerto de Santa María, Sanlúcar de Barrameda, and there sherry has been made for centuries. There are two main types of sherry, *fino* and *oloroso*. The *finos,* which are light bodied and dry, are the choice for an aperitif, while the full-bodied, richly flavored *olorosos* are typically served with main courses, or if sweetened, as a dessert wine.

Sherry is a fortified white wine made primarily from one grape variety, the Palomino, and then aged in oak casks. The method of aging, known as the *solera* system, is unique to sherry making, however. Barrels full of sherry—and each may contain as much as 150 gallons—are stacked in tiers, pyramid style, in large white buildings called *bodegas*, with a new tier added each year. Only when the *solera* has been fully established, that is, when it has reached its complete complement of tiers, can the wine be drawn off. Then, at least twice a year, about 20 percent of the sherry in the bottom tier is

BEAUMES-DE-VENISE

FINO SHERRY WITH DATES AND PARMESAN

siphoned off and replaced immediately with sherry from the next tier up, and the process continues throughout the pyramid. Because barrels of wine have been set aside for each *solera*, the progression through the tiers continues indefinitely, as new barrels replace those now emptied. The drawn sherry may then undergo a further blending process, depending upon the type and style, before it is bottled.

The *finos* are Manzanilla, Fino, and Amontillado. The first two are pale, the clear color of new hay, and very dry. Manzanilla, which can only be made in the seaside town of Sanlúcar de Barrameda, is even lighter than the Fino, and seems to taste of the sea itself. Both pair splendidly with salty, oily fish, nuts, and olives, all of which, in various combinations, are a part of the *tapas* served with *finos* throughout Spain. Amontillado is an aged *fino*, a deep amber-gold, full-bodied and intensely flavored, although it may be dry or slightly sweet, depending upon the style of the maker. Rich appetizers such as grilled figs with bacon (page 107) or thick, caramelized onion *confit* (page 129) are good accompaniments.

The Manzanillas and Finos are best served chilled, but the Amontillados should be only cooled. Served two or three ounces in a sherry glass, or substitute a tulip Champagne glass or a brandy snifter, as they, like the sherry glass, capture and direct the aroma, which is such an integral part of the pleasure and appeal of sherry.

When buying or ordering Manzanilla or Fino, inquire when it was bottled, as these sherries should be consumed within six to eight months of bottling. Once opened, recork and place the bottle in the refrigerator, where it will remain at its peak from one to two weeks. An Amontillado stored in the same manner will last a little longer, from two to three weeks.

VERMOUTH

A FORTIFIED WINE BLENDED WITH DOZENS OF HERBS AND SPICES, VERMOUTH HAS ORIGINS THAT REACH BACK INTO ANTIQUITY. IT MAY BE SWEET OR DRY DEPENDING UPON THE COM-bination of ingredients—always secret—and the process used. Even the names of just some of the aromatic elements—violets and roses, hyssop and juniper, oregano and wild thyme, chamomile and cloves, bitter orange and sweet cinnamon—speak of a seduction of the senses, causing each sip to seem as if one were taking in veritable meadows, hillsides, and orchards.

Red or sweet vermouth, once called Italian in order to differentiate it from the dry vermouth made in France, has a rich, round, faintly bitter citrus flavor, while white or dry vermouth has a more delicate herbal and floral taste. The red, really a russet color, comes from the addition of caramel to the final product, rather than from using red wine as a base.

The first commercial vermouth was made in Turin, Italy, in 1786, by an Italian named Carpano, purportedly using a recipe handed down from his grandmother. The venture was successful and Carpano's vermouth began being sold in Italy and France, and also was exported to the United States. Fourteen years later, Joseph Noilly of Lyons, France, created a vermouth that was less sweet than the Italian vermouths, and it was called French, or dry, vermouth. Today, French and Italian firms make both a dry style and a sweet, and the differentiation comes not from nationality, but in the individual manufacturing of the product. Thus, the Italian manufacturer Martini & Rossi makes a sweet vermouth and a dry one, as does Noilly-Prat. The house of Carpano makes a sweet vermouth called Punt e Mes, which is quite distinctly flavored. Other manufacturers of vermouth include the French firm Lejohn and the Italian Cinzano.

Vermouth may be savored *au naturel* or over ice, a twist of lemon with the dry, orange or lemon with the sweet. Dry vermouth is exceptional with sweet dates and dry cheeses such as *pecorino* or Parmesan, while sweet vermouth is fully complemented by the rich flavor of bacon-wrapped figs (page 107) and toasted nuts, almonds or orange-glazed pecans, for example.

Serve at room temperature, pouring two to three ounces into each glass, over ice, if desired. Once opened, recap tightly. Vermouth will keep for up to one year stored in a cool, dark place or refrigerated. Noilly-Prat recommends storing their product in the refrigerator for up to six months.

DUBONNET

I HAVE A PARTICULAR AFFECTION FOR DUBONNET. MY MOTHER USED TO SERVE THE DEEP GARNET APERITIF IN SMALL-CUT GLASS GOBLETS THAT SHE RESERVED FOR SPECIAL OCCASIONS. I loved the way it looked in the glass, and its taste was sweet, like black currants. She had discovered Dubonnet on a trip she made to Europe by ship, a voyage that was one of the high points of her life. It remained for her a liquid symbol of those elegant evenings when she dressed for dinner and dined among glittering people speaking a dozen different languages.

Dubonnet's origins are with a nineteenth-century wine merchant. In the mid–eighteen hundreds, Joseph Dubonnet blended wines and flavored them with quinine and other ingredients to make a creation that he first called Quinquina Dubonnet. So pleased was he with the success of his efforts, he devoted himself to the production of the aperitif, giving up other aspects of the wine business.

A series of different processes combine to make Dubonnet. They include blending the separate juices of both red and white wine grapes whose fermentation has been halted by the addition of alcohol with a number of aromatic herbs and spices. Of course, the full spectrum of ingredients and their proportions remains arcane, but the manufacturer does tell us that such diverse elements as green coffee beans, cinnamon, chamomile, and rinds from the sour Seville orange are among the flavorings, as well as quinine made from the bark of the cinchona tree.

Although perhaps best known in its red version, Dubonnet also exists in white and amber styles, the results of different blends. Dubonnet, in all its versions, is a versatile aperitif that pairs equally well with rich appetizers such as anchovy puffs (page 109) and risotto croquettes (page 126) as it does with *tapenade* toasts (page 106) or plain olives.

Served slightly chilled, or with ice cubes, pouring three ounces into each glass. Once opened, recap tightly and store in the refrigerator for up to three months.

LILLET BLANC

LILLET

LILLET BLANC AND LILLET ROUGE ARE DELICATE, FAINTLY CITRUS-FLAVORED, WINE-BASED APERITIFS MADE IN THE BORDEAUX REGION. THE GENESIS OF LILLET IS ATTRIBUTED TO THE experimentation of Raymond Lillet, who, with his brother Paul, was a fine wine shipper in France during the late eighteen hundreds. Lillet Blanc is made by blending Bordeaux wines made from Sémillon and Sauvignon Blanc grapes together with orange and lemon brandies, to which a flavoring of quinine is added. The whole is then aged in oak barrels. Lillet Rouge is made in the same fashion, but the wine used is a blend of Cabernet Sauvignon and Merlot.

My first taste of Lillet was in a fourteenth-floor apartment overlooking Gramercy Park in New York City, where a Russian-Hungarian friend served it to me along with toasts spread with smoked whitefish from Zabar's delicatessen. It was a memorable combination. Lillet's rounded, voluptuous taste is also perfect for pistachios or, more substantially, risotto croquettes (page 126) full of the richness of their melting cheese.

Serve well chilled, but without ice, as recommended by its manufacturer, pouring three to four ounces into each wineglass, or over ice in a short bistro glass, as it is served at San Francisco's Le Central restaurant. Once opened, the manufacturer recommends to recap tightly and store in the refrigerator, where it will keep for up to one week.

L'AMER PICON

ONE OF THE BITTER, ALCOHOL-BASED APERITIFS, L'AMER PICON, ALSO CALLED SIMPLY PICON, WAS FIRST POPULAR IN THE 1930S AND 1940S. IT IS ENJOYING A NEW VOGUE IN FRANCE TODAY, where it is heralded in restaurants of a certain style as an aperitif of *autrefois*—of former times—to be rediscovered, along with *vin d'orange, vin de noix,* and Suze. Dark brown, bitter, and powerful, Picon is flavored primarily with quinine, the bark from the cinchona tree, as well as with bitter orange and a mélange of herbs.

Picon is served *au naturel,* with sparkling water, soda, or with plain water, at room temperature or, more commonly, with ice cubes, pouring one-and-a-half ounces into each glass. Once opened, recap and store at room temperature or in a cool, dark place for up to one year.

PICON PUNCH

This classic combination popular in southwestern France also has a loyal following in San Francisco's traditional Italian neighborhood of North Beach, where old-timers instruct newcomers on how to make this refreshing aperitif.

2 tablespoons fresh lemon juice
1 ½ teaspoons grenadine
1 ½ ounces L'Amer Picon
seltzer water
1 teaspoon brandy
thin slice of orange or lemon peel

Combine the lemon juice, grenadine, and L'Amer Picon in a shaker and shake well. Strain into a short bistro glass or a short-stemmed wineglass. Fill the glass with seltzer water. Pour the brandy gently onto the surface to "float" it. Serve immediately, garnished with the slice of orange or lemon peel.

MAKES 1 SERVING

SUZE

ANOTHER OF THE BITTER, ALCOHOL-BASED APERITIFS, SUZE OWES BOTH ITS AMBER-GOLD HUE AND ITS INIMICAL FLAVOR TO THE ROOT OF THE YELLOW GENTIAN (*GENTIANA LUTEA*), a perennial plant that grows wild in France's mountainous regions, particularly in the Massif Central and the Alps. Suze tastes sharp and bitter, a flavor rendered from the fresh root during the steeping process, yet the presence of other herbs and spices softens the bitterness to make an intriguing aperitif. An unusual drink for modern tastes, which are more inclined toward the sweet than the bitter, Suze was popular enough in 1912 to inspire Picasso to paint a portrait of it, which eventually graced the Suze label in a special production.

Suze first appeared in 1889, introduced into the French market by a distillery owner, Fernand Moureaux. Although gentian liqueurs, strong infused and sweetened spirits, were well-known and popular, Suze was the first aperitif to be based on gentian. Unlike the homemade *vin de gentiane* (see page 36), which uses dried gentian root, Suze is produced from the fresh root. I like it with salty peanuts or chips, green olives, or the more elegant onion *confit* (page 129).

Suze may be savored over ice cubes *au naturel.* Like white wine, it may be mixed with *crème de cassis,* which slightly sweetens its distinctive taste. It may also be served at cool room temperature in short-stemmed wineglasses or heavy-bottomed bistro glasses, or combined with plain or sparkling water, in tall glasses with ice cubes, pouring 2 ounces Suze and 4 ounces water into each glass. Once opened, recap tightly and store at room temperature or in a cool, dark place for up to one year.

SUZE AU NATUREL

Put ice cubes in a short glass and pour the Suze over them.

1 or 2 ice cubes
2 ounces Suze

MAKES 1 SERVING

SUZE AND TONIC

Put the ice cubes in a tall glass, add the Suze, then the tonic, and stir.

2 or 3 ice cubes
2 ounces Suze
4 ounces tonic, chilled

MAKES 1 SERVING

SUZE WITH CRÈME DE CASSIS

Put the ice cubes in a short glass, add the Suze, then the *crème de cassis*, and stir.

2 or 3 ice cubes
2 ounces Suze
1 tablespoon crème de cassis

MAKES 1 SERVING

CAMPARI

ONE OF THE MOST DISTINCTIVE ELEMENTS OF CAMPARI, LABELED BITTER CAMPARI OR APER-ITIVO CAMPARI, IS ITS PURE RED HUE. IT HAS A SPICY FLAVOR WITH AN UNDERLYING TRACE of bitter orange, one of the many components used in its manufacturing. Its beginnings lie in the basement of a café in Milan, Italy, where in the 1860s a bartender named Gaspare Campari devised concoctions, among them the one that would bear his family name and be sold worldwide.

Campari is meant to be drunk chilled, icy to the lips. It is commonly served *au naturel* over ice or with ice and soda, and although mixed drinks are not the subject of this book, it should be noted that Campari figures in at least 150 different mixed drinks, the most famous being the Negroni, named for the Italian count credited with its invention. Made with gin, sweet vermouth, and bitters, it resembles another famous Campari drink, the Americano, which is made in the same fashion but with a slice of lemon instead of bitters. Campari also markets an alcohol-free aperitif labeled Americano.

This popular spirit is created by macerating herbs in water and alcohol to create an infusion that is then blended with more alcohol and sugar to create the final drink. The astonishing color comes not from the flavoring ingredients, but from cochineal, a natural colorant.

Partner Campari with cracked green olives from a brine flavored with dried orange peel, or with the basic flavors of salted nuts. For something more elaborate, toasts spread with salt cod *brandade* (page 128), or bite-sized portions of still-warm onion tart (page 114) are good choices.

Serve chilled over ice, pouring two to three ounces into each short glass. Once opened, recap tightly and store in a cool, dark place or at room temperature for up to one year.

CAMPARI AND SODA

3 or 4 ice cubes

2 ounces Campari

2 ounces soda water, or to taste, chilled

thin slice of orange or lemon peel (optional)

Put the ice cubes in a tall chilled glass, and pour the Campari over them. Pour in the soda water, stir, and add the citrus peel as a garnish, if desired. Serve at once.

MAKES 1 SERVING

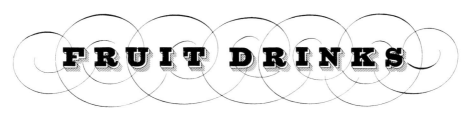

FRUIT DRINKS

FRUIT-BASED DRINKS, WHETHER MADE WITH FRESH FRUIT OR WITH FRUIT SYRUPS, ARE NONALCOHOLIC BEVERAGES CHOSEN, LIKE other aperitifs, to sharpen the senses for the meal to come. Lemons, limes, and other citrus used in various preparations and combinations bring tartness and acidity to their beverages, as does pineapple to a lesser degree. Tomatoes, technically fruits, are treated as savories when seasoned with salt, pepper, perhaps basil or other herbs, and served as a juice. Ice can be an integral component of fruit drinks when crushed and then swirled with juice or syrup to make a slush.

Concentrated fruit syrups in a lush pantheon of flavors lend their intense taste to still water, lemonade, and sparkling mineral water to make a tantalizing aperitif. Several brands of good-quality syrups are available and only a small amount of syrup is needed to make a simple, yet flavorful drink. More complex and exotic versions may be made by adding fresh fruit, sprigs of herbs, or crushed ice to the basic drink.

Obviously many excellent fruit drinks may be purchased ready-made, and the combinations available are continually expanding. More now are made using only fruits and vegetables that have been organically grown, and an increasing number of tropical fruits are being bottled in mixed flavors; mango and melon and guava, pineapple, and passion fruit are just two of the growing lexicon of blended juices. It is difficult, though, to capture the seasonal flavor and taste delivered by a glass of orange juice freshly squeezed, of homemade lemonade, or of tomato juice crushed from garden-fresh tomatoes. Supplies of exotic mangoes, papayas, cherimoyas, and guavas from the tropics along with such staples as bananas and pineapples allow us to blend and purée our own creations. Citrus juices are easily made using the simplest of manual juicers or reamers. Powerful electric juicers, which crush and then separate juice from pulp, are needed to extract the juice from cucumbers and fennel, from carrots and apples, and from other fruits and vegetables that are too fibrous, too hard, or otherwise unsuitable for juicing by hand or in a blender.

The salty triumvirate of olives, nuts, and crackers—foods that quicken the appetite just as the aperitif itself does—generally complements fruit-based drinks. These fruit beverages, especially the sweet ones, are also amenable to spicy bites of sausage or chili. But use culinary caution when pairing the sweeter drinks with some of the sweeter foods such as a caramelized onion *confit* (page 129), for the similar tastes may battle rather than enhance each other.

MEDLEY OF CITRUS

CITRON PRESSÉ

ONE OF THE MOST ELEGANT OF THE FRUIT APERITIF DRINKS, *CITRON PRESSÉ* IS SERVED IN CAFÉS — AND IN HOMES, TOO — WITH RITUAL AND ACCOUTREMENTS THAT SET THE STAGE FOR the eventual meal. The glass is tall, the spoon is long-handled, the lemon served with a small glass reamer and a strainer. They are accompanied with a pitcher of water, a bowl of ice cubes with tongs, and a bowl of sugar with a spoon. Everything necessary for preparing the drink to the individual taste is at hand. The process begins: First the lemon is reamed. The strainer is put atop the glass and the juice is poured through it. Water is added to the juice and then it is stirred, sampled, and the proportion is corrected. Sugar contributes the desired amount of sweetness, and more sampling occurs. Lastly, a few ice cubes clink into the glass. With a final stirring, the *citron presse* is acceptable. Of course, the drink can be prepared by the pitcherful, but I find the anticipatory aspect of the tableside preparation quite conducive to the transition to sociability that is the hallmark of an aperitif.

Because the sweetness is adjusted to individual taste, the fact that some lemons are considerably sweeter than others is not as relevant as it is when general measurements are given. Meyer lemons, especially when left a long time on the tree, may be so sweet that only a dash of sugar is needed; the more readily available Eureka and Lisbon lemons are more acidic and tart, and so more sugar is needed. *Citron presse* is so dominated by the acidity of the fresh lemon juice, however, that no matter how much sugar is added, it will never acquire the smooth, sweet taste of lemonade made with a sugar syrup. *Citrons verts,* or limes, may be prepared in this same way, although two or three limes, depending upon their juiciness, may be required per serving.

Rosemary-walnut *biscotti* (page 117), *petits farcis* (page 118), and salted nuts demonstrate the range of food choices that can be served with *citron presse.*

1 lemon, any kind, halved

1 to 1½ cups cold water

2 to 6 tablespoons granulated sugar

ice cubes

fresh lemon verbena or lemon thyme sprig (optional)

Cut the lemon in half and ream or squeeze the juice from the halves. Pour the juice through a small strainer set over a tall glass. Add the water, about ¾ cup for an intense lemon taste, up to 1½ cups for a light lemon taste. Add the sugar according to your taste. Drop in the ice cubes and garnish with the herb sprig, if desired.

MAKES 1 SERVING

LIMEADE

A TALL LIMEADE, LIKE LEMONADE, IS A DELICIOUS THIRST QUENCHER AND WONDERFUL PRE- LUDE TO A MEAL, ESPECIALLY WHEN IT HAS BEEN FRESHLY MADE AND IS NOT AS CLOY- ingly sweet as some commercially made ades. Freshly squeezed juice is added to a light sugar-syrup base, the whole combining flavors that are equally balanced.

Cut the limes in half and ream or squeeze the juice from them. Pour the juice through a fine-mesh sieve into a measuring cup and discard the seeds and the pulp. You should have ½ cup. Cover and refrigerate.

*6 to 8 limes, enough to
yield ½ cup juice*

4 cups water

¾ cup granulated sugar

½ teaspoon salt

ice cubes (optional)

fresh mint sprigs (optional)

Place the water, sugar, and salt in a saucepan and bring to a boil over medium-high heat, stirring often. Boil, continuing to stir, until the sugar has dissolved and a light syrup has formed, about 2 minutes. Remove from the heat, let cool, cover, and refrigerate until well chilled.

Pour the chilled syrup into a pitcher, add the lime juice, and stir well. Taste and adjust for sugar. Pour into glasses. If desired, serve with ice cubes, and garnish with sprigs of mint.

MAKES FOUR 8-OUNCE SERVINGS

STRAWBERRY LEMONADE

L EMONADE, OFTEN FLAVORED WITH VARIOUS SEASONAL FRUITS, WAS A MAINSTAY OF FRENCH BOURGEOIS HOMES IN THE NINETEENTH CENTURY AND INTO THE TWENTIETH. LEMONADE sets consisting of a rack with a carrying handle that held a carafe surrounded by six or eight glasses were an important part of a proper household.

Lemonade is made like limeade: a light sugar syrup is made first and the lemon juice is added to it. Here, the lemonade is given a strawberry flavoring by adding the fresh berries during the syrup-making process. The result is a drink with a delicate pink color and a sweet berry finish. The recipe is easily varied by using raspberries or black currants, for example. Or you can cheat a little and use purchased fruit syrup for flavoring.

3 or 4 lemons, enough to yield ½ cup juice

4 cups water

¾ cup granulated sugar

½ teaspoon salt

1 cup strawberries, hulled

ice cubes (optional)

thin lemon slices (optional)

Cut the lemons in half and ream or squeeze the juice from them. Pour the juice through a fine-mesh sieve into a measuring cup and discard the seeds and the pulp. You should have ½ cup. Cover and refrigerate.

Place the water, sugar, salt, and strawberries in a saucepan and bring to a boil over medium-high heat. As the mixture heats, stir it often with a wooden spoon and, using the back of the spoon, crush the berries. Continue to boil, stirring often, until the sugar has dissolved and a light syrup has formed, about 2 minutes. Remove from the heat, let cool, cover, and refrigerate until well chilled.

Pour the chilled syrup through a fine-mesh sieve into a pitcher; discard all the strawberry pulp. Add the lemon juice and stir well. Taste and adjust for sugar.

Pour into glasses. Serve with ice cubes and garnish with lemon slices, if desired.

MAKES FOUR 8 OUNCE SERVINGS

LEMON-LIME SLUSH

*T*ART AND TANGY, THIS DRINK REMINDS ME OF THE HOMEMADE SNOW CONES OF MY CHILDHOOD THAT WERE NEVER AS SWEET AS THE SYRUP ONES WE BOUGHT AT THE COUNTRY FAIR. A SIMple whirring and slurring of ice and juice in a blender produces the slush, and the juices of oranges, grapefruits, and the more exotic citrus such as limequats or kumquats may be used instead of the lemon-lime combination.

10 limes, enough to yield
½ cup juice

3 or 4 lemons, enough to yield
½ cup juice

1 to 3 tablespoons granulated sugar

3 ice cubes, crushed

fresh mint sprig (optional)

The quantity of fruits needed to make the slush will depend not only upon their size, but also their juiciness. Limes may vary from yielding one tablespoon to double that amount, and a thin-skinned, sweet Meyer lemon will give as much as a quarter of a cup, but a thicker-skinned Lisbon lemon will give less. The tangy sweet taste of lemon-lime is ideal to complement spicy appetizers.

Cut the limes and lemons in half and ream or squeeze the juice from them; keep the juices separate. Pour each juice through a fine-mesh sieve and discard the seeds and the pulp. You should have ½ cup of each juice. Taste and add the sugar according to your taste. (Note: Sweet Meyer lemons will require less sugar than the more tart varieties.)

Place the reserved juice in a blender with the ice cubes and blend until slushy. Pour into a tall glass and serve immediately, garnished with a mint sprig, if desired, and accompanied with a long-handled spoon.

MAKES 1 SERVING

PINEAPPLE SLUSH

2 cups cubed fresh pineapple
3 or 4 ice cubes, crushed

Put the pineapple in a blender with the ice cubes and blend until slushy. Pour into a tall glass and serve immediately, accompanied with a long-handled spoon.

MAKES 1 SERVING

PAPAYA AND PINEAPPLE JUICE

THIS IS A BASIC BLENDER DRINK WITH FLAVORS BALANCED BETWEEN THE RICHNESS OF THE PAPAYA AND THE SPRIGHTLY BITE OF THE PINEAPPLE. THE TEXTURE, ALTHOUGH DENSER THAN pineapple juice alone, is smooth and flowing. Salty chips and nuts, as well as spicy foods are good choices to serve with this juice.

½ pineapple, peeled, cored, and cut into cubes (approximately 2 cups)

1 medium-sized papaya, peeled, halved, seeded, and cut into cubes (approximately 1 cup)

1 tablespoon fresh lime juice

Put all the ingredients in a blender and process until smooth. Pour into glasses and serve immediately.

MAKES APPROXIMATELY 2 CUPS, 2 SERVINGS

TOMATO JUICE

THE TOMATO IS AMERICA'S FAVORITE VEGETABLE, BUT NOT ITS FAVORITE JUICE, PERHAPS BECAUSE OF ITS THICK TEXTURE. THOSE WHO LIKE IT, THOUGH, *REALLY* LIKE IT, OFTEN SEA-soned with salt and pepper, a dash of Worcestershire, or even hot-pepper sauce. Salty crackers, crunchy raw cucumbers, sweet peppers, chips, olives—all harmonize with tomato juice.

Making tomato juice at home opens up the possibility of selecting the kind and color of tomato to use. Low-acid supersweet and high-acid tart tomatoes each produce a different juice. Color may be

varied as well, since golden yellow, pink, and even white or green-striped specimens are available at summertime farmers' markets, or may be grown in the garden from specialty seeds. Adding basil, jalapeño chilies, sweet bell peppers, fresh ginger, or other inspirations to tomato juice can create a tantalizing array of distinctively flavored aperitifs.

Although tomato juice may be made in a blender, a juicer is more effective for two reasons: it thoroughly emulsifies the liquid, and one can incorporate other ingredients that require juicing, such as fennel, cucumber, and sweet peppers.

TOMATO JUICE WITH BASIL

3 large or 4 medium-sized ripe tomatoes, any color (about 1 pound)

4 fresh basil leaves, plus basil sprigs for garnish

salt and freshly ground black pepper

Core the tomatoes and cut each one into 3 or 4 pieces. Place them and the basil leaves in a juicer. Process according to the manufacturer's instructions. Pour into glasses and serve immediately, garnished with the basil sprigs. Pass the salt and pepper.

MAKES APPROXIMATELY 1 ½ CUPS, 2 SERVINGS

TOMATO, CUCUMBER, AND SWEET PEPPER JUICE

3 large or 4 medium-sized ripe tomatoes (about 1 pound), any color, cored

1 cucumber, peeled and seeded

1 sweet green pepper such as a bell, or a spicier one such as an Anaheim, seeded and deribbed

thin lemon slices

salt and freshly ground black pepper

Cut the tomatoes, cucumber, and green pepper each into 3 or 4 pieces and place them in a juicer. Process according to the manufacturer's instructions. Pour into glasses and serve immediately, garnished with the lemon slices. Pass the salt and pepper.

MAKES APPROXIMATELY 1 ¾ CUPS, 2 OR 3 SERVINGS

FRUIT SYRUPS

*E*SSENCES DERIVED FROM FRUITS, NUTS, OR HERBS FLAVOR A NUMBER OF DIFFERENT BRANDS OF COMMERCIALLY MADE SYRUPS. POPULARIZED IN THE ESPRESSO BARS AND COFFEEHOUSES OF North America as Italian sodas, these syrups are old-time favorites in France, Italy, Spain, and elsewhere in Europe where they are manufactured. As many as thirty-five different flavors are available, and they can be added to still water as well as to soda water, sparkling mineral water, or lemonade for a refreshing aperitif. These resulting drinks are especially appealing to children, and throughout France at aperitif time, youngsters can be heard requesting *menthe à l'eau*. Forthwith, a glass appears filled with a bright green mixture of mint and water, or if mint syrup *sans colorant* has been used, the liquid will show only the palest tinge, if any, of color.

Since no refrigeration is necessary, even after a bottle has been opened, and only water is needed to prepare the drink, fruit-flavored syrups are good items to have in the pantry to offer children and others who prefer a nonalcoholic aperitif. Every French household seems to have on hand at least two or three different syrups with, in my experience, orange, mint, black currant, lemon, and almond the most popular.

The amount of syrup added can be adjusted to individual preferences. Thus, if only a hint of raspberry is wanted, a teaspoon is enough for a water glass, but for deep strawberry, a tablespoon or more would be needed.

MENTHE À L'EAU

1 tablespoon mint syrup
¾ to 1 cup cold water
3 or 4 ice cubes

Put the mint syrup in a glass, add the water, and stir. Add the ice cubes and serve.

MAKES 1 SERVING

FRAMBOISE AU PERRIER

1 tablespoon raspberry syrup

¾ to 1 cup Perrier or other sparkling mineral water, chilled

3 or 4 ice cubes

thin lemon slice

Put the raspberry syrup in a glass, add the mineral water, and stir. Add the ice cubes, garnish with the lemon slice, and serve.

MAKES 1 SERVING

MEDLEY OF CITRUS

GRAPEFRUITS, BLOOD ORANGES, AND NAVEL ORANGES ARE ALL IN SEASON AT THE SAME TIME IN WINTER, WHICH MAKES COMBINING THEM INTO A SEASONAL APERITIF DRINK APPROPRIATE. Grapefruits contribute their tartness, blood oranges the garnet color and sweet berry flavor, and the navels the pure taste of sweet, ripe oranges.

Using a manual or electric reamer or juicer, extract the juice from the citrus fruits. Strain the juice through a fine-mesh sieve into a pitcher and discard the seeds and the pulp. Pour into glasses and serve immediately.

2 grapefruits
4 blood oranges
4 navel oranges

MAKES APPROXIMATELY 1 QUART, 4 SERVINGS

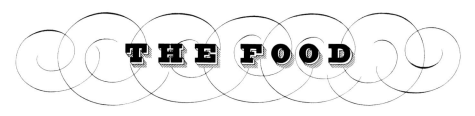

THE FOOD

THERE ARE MANY DIFFERENT FOODS THAT ARE APPROPRIATE FOR SERVING WITH APERITIFS. GENERALLY SIMPLE, EASY TO EAT WITH YOUR your fingers, these *amuse-gueules*—mouth-ticklers—are traditionally small bites, often salty. Nuts, olives, savory spreads and pastries, crunchy raw vegetables, tiny clams or mussels are among the classics that suit virtually any aperitif, from white wine to complex blends and infusions such as *pastis* or Lillet. Dried fruits, foie gras, spiced and sugared nuts, and other appetizers prepared with varied ingredients lend themselves to more precise matching and experimentation. The richness of foie gras is complemented by Champagne, and the sensibility of intensely sweet Medjool dates and slices of Parmesan soars with sips of sweet vermouth or a medium-dry sherry.

When the aperitif is taken at the table in a restaurant setting or at home, a more elaborate appetizer, such as an *anchoïade* with a selection of raw vegetables or a *galette* of wild mushrooms, requiring a knife and fork, might be served. A terrine filled with a spread of *tapenade* and surrounded by toasts may be set in the center of a restaurant table, but in a more casual setting the toasts might be passed already prepared.

Fresh fava beans, peas, and tiny radishes, all seasonal specialties, appear with a saucer of salt in both casual and formal settings. Popped from their pods, the favas and peas are dipped in the salt and eaten singly. As the conversation flows, the aperitifs are sipped, and the pile of empty pods grows. Radishes, grasped by their foliage, are dunked in the salt and munched until only the leaves remain.

Whether it is raw vegetables, nuts, puff pastries, or foie gras, Champagne or *pastis, vin maison* or sherry, empty glasses and desolate plates and bowls signal that the prelude is now over and the palate primed for the meal to come.

TOASTED ALMONDS OR PISTACHIOS

LTHOUGH NUTS OF ALL KINDS ARE AMONG THE BEST ACCOMPANIMENTS TO AN APERITIF, THE ADDED CRUNCH, COLOR, AND FAINTLY SMOKY TASTES THAT NUTS ACQUIRE WHEN toasted further intensify the complementary partnership. The toasting can be done in the oven or in a skillet on the stovetop. In both instances, they key is to toast, not to burn!

Preheat an oven to 300 degrees F.

1 cup shelled almonds, skins intact, or unshelled pistachios

Spread the nuts in a single layer on a baking sheet. Place them in the oven and cook for approximately 30 minutes, stirring from time to time. To test for doneness, remove a nut from the baking sheet and bite into it; the interior should be toasted to a light golden brown. Remove and let stand 5 minutes before serving.

MAKES 1 CUP, 6 SERVINGS

HOMEMADE CHIPS

HIN, CRISPY POTATO CHIPS, ALONG WITH OLIVES, ARE A PERENNIAL FAVORITE TO ACCOMPANY AN APERITIF. FOR VARIATION, TRY USING POTATOES OF DIFFERENT COLORS OR SWEET POTATOES. The latter make delicious, slightly sweet bites.

2 large russet potatoes or blue potatoes, or 2 medium-to-large sweet potatoes

peanut oil or canola oil for deep-frying

salt

Peel the potatoes or not, depending upon whether you want a casual or more formal look. Slice the potatoes as thinly as possible. A French slicer, the mandoline, adjusts to make paper-thin pieces—not even ⅛ inch thick—which are ideal. Place the slices in cold water as they are cut. They will keep thusly for several hours.

In a deep-fat fryer or heavy-bottomed skillet or saucepan, pour in the oil to a depth of 3 inches. Heat to approximately 350 degrees F on a deep-fat frying thermometer, or until a drop of water added to the oil pops.

Drain the potato slices and dry thoroughly. Add them to the oil, a few at a time, removing them with a basket or slotted spoon as soon as they are golden brown; only a minute or two are needed. Place the chips between layers of absorbent paper towels and pat dry. Repeat until all the chips are fried.

Sprinkle lightly with salt. Serve hot, warm, or at room temperature.

MAKES 4 SERVINGS

THREE OLIVES

THROUGHOUT THE MEDITERRANEAN, DOZENS OF OLIVE VARIETIES, CURED AND SEASONED IN EQUALLY NUMEROUS DIFFERENT WAYS, ARE AVAILABLE EVERYWHERE. IN SOME SPECIALTY markets here it is possible to locate an array of interesting olives. If you have difficulty finding such a place, here are some suggestions for seasoning your own olives.

1 jar or can (8 ounces) green olives with or without pits

½ lemon, cut into small pieces

1 dried bay leaf, crumbled

1 tablespoon whole black peppercorns

¼ teaspoon salt

¼ cup cold-pressed extra-virgin olive oil

GREEN OLIVES WITH LEMON AND BAY

Drain the olives and discard the brine in which they were packed. Put them in a small bowl and add all the remaining ingredients. Turn the olives to coat them. Cover the bowl and let the olives marinate in the refrigerator for a week before serving. Stored in the refrigerator, they will keep for a month or longer; after 2 weeks, remove and discard the lemon.

MAKES 1 CUP

SPICY BLACK OLIVES

1 jar or can (8 ounces) black olives with or without pits

4 cloves garlic, crushed

3 to 5 small dried red chilies such as árbol, pequin, or bird's eye

1 teaspoon dried thyme

2 tablespoons small white cocktail onions

1 teaspoon whole black peppercorns

¼ teaspoon salt

¼ cup cold-pressed extra-virgin olive oil

Drain the olives and discard the brine in which they were packed. Put them in a small bowl and add all the remaining ingredients. Turn the olives to coat them. Cover the bowl and let the olives marinate in the refrigerator for a week before serving. Stored in the refrigerator, they will keep for a month or longer; after 2 weeks, remove and discard the garlic and chilies.

MAKES 1 CUP

CRACKED GREEN OLIVES WITH FENNEL

1 jar or can (8 ounces) green olives with pits

1 teaspoon fennel seeds

1 piece orange zest, about 3 inches long and ½ inch wide

¼ cup fresh tarragon leaves

¼ teaspoon salt

¼ cup cold-pressed extra-virgin olive oil

Drain the olives and discard the brine in which they were packed. With the back of a wooden spoon, press each olive just hard enough to crack it open. Do not remove the pits. Put the olives in a small bowl and add all the remaining ingredients. Turn the olives to coat them. Cover the bowl and let the olives marinate in the refrigerator for a week before serving. Stored in the refrigerator, they will keep for a month or longer.

MAKES 1 CUP

FRESH FAVAS AND PEAS IN THEIR PODS

ONLY THE TINIEST, YOUNGEST FAVA BEANS ARE SUITABLE FOR EATING RAW. THEY SHOULD BE NO LARGER AROUND THAN THE TIP OF A LITTLE FINGER. AS THE BEANS MATURE, THE OUTER skin becomes tough and too bitter for most tastes. Half the fun of serving favas in their pods is the opening of the pods. By bending back then pulling the tip of the stem, the pod opens to reveal

1 pound fava beans, unshelled

1 pound English peas, unshelled

salt

a row of six or seven delicate beans snugly couched in a soft, cottony lining. The beans can be plucked out, dipped in salt, and savored. English pea pods, though lacking the plush lining of the fava beans, are equally fun to strip open. Each pea is attached to the pod by a minuscule stem, so that the tender spheres can be picked out precisely, one by one.

Pile the beans and peas in a bowl. Place salt in a small saucer. Set them all out on a table for guests to eat at their leisure.

MAKES 8 SERVINGS

YOUNG RADISHES AND BUTTER

A TRULY CLASSIC FRENCH COMBINATION, RADISHES AND BUTTER ARE AS LIKELY TO APPEAR ON THE LINEN-TOPPED TABLE OF A RESTAURANT AS ON THE KNEE OF A SHEPHERD WITH his just-opened midday knapsack. Select young, tender radishes, either the white-tipped French breakfast type or other comparable varieties. Large, fully mature radishes may develop pithiness and be too intensely peppery to enjoy with an aperitif.

16 young radishes, greens intact

¼ pound unsalted butter

8 to 12 fresh and crusty baguette slices

salt

Remove the largest and any discolored leaves from the radishes, but keep intact the young, bright green leaves. Clip the thin root, but do not cut into the body of the radish. For casual occasions, I leave the root uncut, too. Serve the radishes with the butter, bread, and a saucer of salt for dipping.

MAKES 4 SERVINGS

DATES AND PARMESAN

THE SWEET, THE DRY, AND THE SALTY—ALL COMBINE TO MAKE A PLEASING TASTE SENSATION THAT ALTHOUGH TYPICALLY SERVED AT THE END OF THE MEAL, CAN BE EQUALLY ENJOYED AT the beginning with an aperitif. Medium-dry sherry, homemade lemonade, and sweet *vin cuit,* though quite different in flavor, are all complemented by this combination of dried fruit and cheese.

My preferred date is the large, rich, and densely sweet Medjool, but any flavorful dates will suffice. The Parmesan should be well aged and of a good quality.

8 dates

2 ounces Parmesan cheese, cut into the thinnest slices

Serve the dates and the cheese together on a single serving plate, or for a more formal occasion, 2 dates and 1 or 2 slices of cheese per person on 4 individual plates.

MAKES 4 SERVINGS

BLACK OLIVE TAPENADE

A BASIC SPREAD FOR GRILLED TOASTS IN SOUTHERN FRANCE, *TAPENADE* IS MADE IN MANY DIFFERENT WAYS: WITH AND WITHOUT ANCHOVIES, WITH AND WITHOUT GARLIC, WITH and without bread crumbs, and with various other additions and omissions, but nearly always with capers. *Tapenade* is a welcome partner for any aperitif, from Champagne to lemonade.

½ pound Mediterranean-style black olives

5 olive oil packed anchovy fillets or well-rinsed salt-packed ones

1 tablespoon drained capers

½ teaspoon minced fresh thyme

1 teaspoon fresh lemon juice

1 or 2 tablespoons olive oil

With the back of a wooden spoon, press each olive hard enough to break it open, then remove the pit. Put the pitted olives, anchovies, capers, thyme, and lemon juice in a blender and process until a paste forms. Add the olive oil, a little at a time, until the paste is smooth but not oily. Or, if you prefer, make the spread in the traditional way using a mortar and pestle, grinding the ingredients together one by one.

If not serving immediately, put the *tapenade* in a covered jar and store in the refrigerator, where it will keep for up to 3 months.

MAKES APPROXIMATELY ½ CUP

DRIED FIGS WITH BACON AND FRESH GOAT CHEESE

CHEWY SWEET FIGS COMBINE WITH THE CRISP SALTINESS OF BACON AND THE SOFT TEXTURE OF GOAT CHEESE TO FORM A HARMONIOUS WHOLE. DRIED PRUNES MAY BE TREATED IN THE SAME way with an equally successful result, and different cheeses may be used, such as Gorgonzola or feta. Choose figs (or prunes) that are supple and have retained their natural shapes, not those that are hard or flattened, as the latter do not lend themselves to being stuffed. These nibbles are particularly nice with full-bodied aperitifs such as sweet vermouth, *vin de noix,* and Beaumes-de-Venise or other muscat wines. They also complement the anise-flavored aperitifs.

12 dried figs such as Mission

¼ pound fresh goat cheese, divided into 12 equal portions

2 or 3 slices bacon, cut into 2-inch-long pieces, to total 12 pieces

Preheat a broiler. Make a lengthwise slit in each fig. Tuck a portion of cheese into each slit, then wrap with a piece of bacon and secure closed with a toothpick.

Arrange on a broiler pan and slip into the broiler. Broil, turning once, just until the bacon is browned and barely crisped. Serve hot or warm.

MAKES 3 OR 4 SERVINGS

ROASTED RED PEPPER SPREAD

ROASTED RED PEPPERS, PACKED IN HERBED OLIVE OIL, CAN BE TURNED QUICKLY INTO A TASTY SPREAD FOR TOASTS BY SIMPLY PURÉEING THEM IN A BLENDER. THEIR SMOKY TASTE goes especially well with *vin de noix*, dry vermouth, and medium-dry white wines.

Preheat an oven to 500 degrees F, preheat a broiler, or prepare a fire in a charcoal grill. Arrange the sweet peppers in a shallow pan, on a broiler tray, or on a grill rack, and roast, broil, or grill, turning the peppers so they color evenly, until blackened on all sides, 3 to 4 minutes on each side. Slip the peppers into a plastic bag and close the top. Let stand to allow the skins to steam and loosen, 4 to 5 minutes. Remove the peppers from the bag and slip off the blackened skins. Gently pull or cut out the stems. Make a single lengthwise slit in each pepper and remove the seeds and ribs.

1 pound thick-fleshed sweet red peppers such as bell or pimiento

½ teaspoon salt

1 teaspoon freshly ground black pepper

2 cloves garlic

2 teaspoons minced fresh rosemary

2 tablespoons olive oil

Place the peppers in a glass or ceramic bowl or jar and add the salt, black pepper, garlic, and rosemary. Pour in the olive oil, and turn the peppers to coat them. At this point, they may be covered and refrigerated for several days before puréeing.

When ready to purée, place the contents of the bowl in a blender and purée to make a thin paste. Taste and adjust for seasonings before serving.

MAKES APPROXIMATELY ¾ CUP

ANCHOVY PUFFS

*T*HESE AIRY, CRUSTY, GOLDEN BITE-SIZED SQUARES, TOPPED WITH JUST ENOUGH ANCHOVY TO GIVE A BURST OF THE INIMICABLE TASTE OF THE FISH, ARE ELEGANT YET EASY-TO-MAKE NIBbles if using prepared puff pastry. In France, fresh ready-to-use puff pastry is sold in all the supermarkets in the same section as fresh pasta, but in the United States it is more likely found in the frozen-food section of specialty stores. The richness of the pastry and the tang of the anchovies make these appetizers suitable for serving with most aperitifs, whether bitter or sweet.

4 ounces olive oil–packed anchovy fillets

4 tablespoons cold-press extra-virgin olive oil

6 cloves garlic

1 sheet prepared puff pastry, 10 by 12 inches and ¼ inch thick, thawed if frozen

¼ cup minced fresh thyme

Remove the anchovy fillets from the oil and cut them into small pieces. Set aside. In a small bowl, combine the olive oil with the garlic cloves. Using the back of a fork, mash them together to make a paste.

Cut the pastry into 1-inch squares, making 120 squares in all. With a pastry brush, spread the squares with the oil and garlic paste. Top each square with a piece or two of anchovy and a pinch of thyme. Place on an ungreased baking sheet. Bake at 350 degrees F until the tops have turned golden brown and the pastry has risen to almost an inch high, 25 to 30 minutes.

Serve hot or at room temperature.

MAKES 120 PUFFS, 30 SERVINGS

GOUGÈRE

GOUGÈRE IS FORMED FROM THE SAME DOUGH AS A CREAM PUFF, BUT WITH THE ADDITION OF CHEESE. QUITE EASY TO MAKE, TINY *GOUGÈRES* ARE ONE OF THE MOST POPULAR *AMUSE-gueules.* They may be eaten plain, or slit open and filled with a teaspoon of such savory fillings as *brandade* of salt cod (page 128), minced shrimp and green peppers, or salmon roe mixed with *mascarpone* cheese. Their elegant appearance makes them appropriate for serving with Champagne, but they are agreeable companions for virtually any aperitif.

1 cup water

6 ½ tablespoons unsalted butter

1 teaspoon salt

¼ teaspoon cayenne pepper

1 cup all-purpose flour

4 eggs

¼ cup finely grated Parmesan cheese

¼ cup finely grated Gruyère cheese

1 egg beaten with 1 teaspoon water

In a heavy-bottomed, medium-sized saucepan, bring the water, 6 tablespoons of the butter, salt, and cayenne pepper to a boil over medium-high heat. Boil until butter melts, then remove from heat. Pour in the flour, beating for a few moments with a wooden spoon to blend and bind the ingredients. Return to medium-high heat and continue to beat vigorously until the mixture pulls away from the sides of the pan and holds together, about 2 minutes.

Again remove the saucepan from the heat. Make a well in the center of the paste and break an egg into it. Beat to incorporate the egg. Repeat until all 4 eggs have been added and the mixture has become a smooth paste. Now beat in all of the Parmesan and half of the Gruyère.

Preheat an oven to 425 degrees F. Butter a baking sheet with the remaining ½ tablespoon butter.

Fill a cup with hot water. Dip a tablespoon first into the hot water and then into the pastry. Using your finger, or another spoon, push the spoonful of pastry onto the baking sheet. Repeat, spacing the puffs about 2 inches apart. Using a pastry brush, coat only the top surface of the puff with the egg-water mixture. Do not allow the egg mixture to dribble down the sides or it will bind the pastry to the baking sheet and prevent puffing. Sprinkle each puff with a few shreds of the reserved Gruyère cheese.

Bake until the puffs are golden brown and have increased in size 1½ times, 20 to 25 minutes. Remove from the oven and pierce each with a skewer to release the steam. Let cool for 10 to 15 minutes before serving (or slitting, if they are going to be stuffed). Serve warm or at room temperature.

MAKES ABOUT 35 PUFFS, EACH ABOUT 1½ INCHES IN DIAMETER, 6 TO 8 SERVINGS

SPICY BLACK BEAN WONTONS

*S*PICY BITES INSIDE CRISP FRIED WONTON WRAPPERS ARE WELL PAIRED WITH FRUITY WINES SUCH AS GERWÜRZTRAMINER, *VIN MARQUIS, VIN D'ORANGE,* SWEET VERMOUTH, AND SEMI-sweet sparkling wines such as Italian *muscato d'Asti.* Homemade limeade and sparkling drinks made with flavored syrups are also good choices.

Combine the beans, water, dried chilies, onion, garlic, salt and black pepper in a saucepan and bring to a boil over medium-high heat. Boil for 2 to 3 minutes, then reduce the heat and simmer, partially covered, until the beans are tender, 1½ to 2 hours. Add additional water if necessary during cooking to keep beans covered by 1 inch. Drain the cooked beans, reserving the cooking liquid. Let cool slightly. Working in batches, purée the beans in a blender, adding the reserved cooking liquid as necessary to produce a thick and slightly moist paste. Transfer to a bowl.

1 cup dried black beans, picked over and rinsed

8 cups water

2 dried chilies such as pasilla or ancho, stemmed and seeded

1 yellow onion, quartered

4 cloves garlic, halved

1 teaspoon salt

1 teaspoon freshly ground black pepper

36 wonton wrappers, 3½ inches in diameter or 3½ inches square

2 or 3 fresh jalapeño chilies, seeded and minced

¼ cup minced fresh cilantro

light oil such as canola for frying

To fill each wonton wrapper, place 1 tablespoon of the puréed beans in the middle of the wrapper. Sprinkle with ⅛ teaspoon of the minced jalapeño and ¼ teaspoon of the minced cilantro. Fold the wrapper over to make a half-moon or a triangle, spreading a little water on the inner edges and pressing together to seal. As the wontons are filled, set them aside on waxed paper and cover with a damp towel to keep them moist until you are ready to cook them.

In a wok or deep skillet, pour in oil to a depth of ½ inch. Heat the oil over medium-high heat until it sizzles when a drop of water hits it. Reduce the heat to medium and, using tongs, place the wontons, a few at a time, into the hot oil. Fry on one side until golden and slightly puffed, about 1 minute. Turn and fry on the other side until golden, 30 to 40 seconds. Using the tongs, remove the wontons, holding each one over the pan for a moment or two to allow any excess oil to drip, and set on paper towels to drain. Repeat until all the wontons are cooked.

Let the wontons cool for 5 minutes, then serve.

MAKES 36 WONTONS, 6 TO 8 SERVINGS

ONION TART

A SAVORY CUSTARD FILLED WITH THE TASTE OF SWEETLY CARAMELIZED ONIONS AND BAKED IN A FLAKY CRUST IS A STAPLE FIRST COURSE IN FRANCE. BUT THE SAME TART CUT INTO small pieces becomes an *amuse-gueule* to serve with the whole array of aperitifs.

Preheat an oven 425 degrees F.

To make the tart shell, sift together the flour and salt into a bowl. Using a pastry blender or two knives, cut the margarine or butter into the flour until small pieces of fat and flour, about the size of peas, have formed. Add the water a teaspoon or two at a time, mixing it into the flour mixture with a fork. Gather the mixture into a ball, pressing gently, and wrap in plastic wrap. Place in the refrigerator to chill for 10 minutes.

Sprinkle a board or a pastry cloth and a rolling pin with a light coating of flour. Place the ball of chilled dough in the middle of the surface and, with your hands, pat it down until it is about 1 inch thick. Using the rolling pin, roll the dough into a ¼-inch-thick round approximately 10 inches in diameter. To move the pastry round to the pie pan, overlap it around the rolling pin, then undrape it over the pie pan. Gently press it into the bottom and sides of the pan and trim the overhanging edges to within ½ inch of the pan rim. Fold the excess under to make a smooth finish and press all around the edge with the tines of a fork. Gently line the pie shell with aluminum foil and add a layer of pie weights or dried beans.

Bake in the preheated oven for 10 minutes. Remove from the oven and take out the weights (or beans) and foil. Prick the bottom all over with the tines of a fork to allow steam to escape. Return to the oven and bake for another 4 to 5 minutes until set. Remove and place on a rack until ready to fill.

Reduce the oven temperature to 375 degrees F.

For the tart shell:

1 cup all-purpose flour

½ teaspoon salt

⅓ cup margarine or ¼ cup unsalted butter, chilled and cut into several pieces

3 tablespoons ice water

For the filling:

2 eggs

⅓ cup heavy cream

⅓ cup half-and-half

1 teaspoon salt

1 teaspoon freshly ground black pepper

½ cup coarsely grated Fontina or Gruyère cheese

1 cup onion confit (page 129)

1 tablespoon all-purpose flour

1 teaspoon minced fresh thyme

1 tablespoon unsalted butter

To make the filling, in a bowl, beat together the eggs, cream, half-and-half, salt, and pepper just to mix. Stir in three-fourths of the cheese. Spread the onion confit on the bottom of the tart shell and sprinkle with the flour and half of the thyme. Pour the egg mixture evenly over the confit. Top with the remaining cheese and then the thyme. Cut the butter into small pieces and dot the surface.

Place in the oven and bake until the top is golden and slightly puffed and a knife inserted into the center comes out clean, about 30 minutes. Remove and let stand on a rack for 10 to 15 minutes before cutting. Cut into pieces about 1½ inches square and serve warm.

MAKES APPROXIMATELY 24 PIECES, 6 TO 8 SERVINGS

ROSEMARY-WALNUT BISCOTTI

*C*RUNCHY, TWICE-COOKED *BISCOTTI* ARE SAVORIES HERE—VERY DENSE AND FULL OF THE TASTE OF WALNUTS. SERVE WITH *VIN DE NOIX* FOR AN UNUSUAL PLAY OF FLAVORS, WITH A *VIN DOUX*, *vin chaud,* or a fruit beverage.

Preheat an oven to 350 degrees F. Butter a baking sheet and lightly dust it with flour.

Combine the flour, finely and coarsely ground nuts, baking soda, salt, pepper, and rosemary in a mixing bowl and turn with a whisk to mix. Make a well in the center and add the eggs. Using a whisk or a hand-held electric beater set on medium speed, incorporate the eggs into the flour mixture to make a stiff, rather sticky dough. With your hands, gather the dough into a ball. Place it on a lightly floured surface and knead it for 2 or 3 minutes until firm. Divide the dough into 2 or 3 equal portions. Using your palms, roll each portion into a log 1½ to 2 inches in diameter.

1¾ cups all-purpose flour

1½ cups finely ground walnuts

¼ cup coarsely ground walnuts

1 teaspoon baking soda

½ teaspoon salt

¼ teaspoon freshly ground black pepper

2 tablespoons minced fresh rosemary

3 eggs, lightly beaten

Place the logs on the prepared baking sheet, spacing them well apart. Bake until the logs have taken on a pale bisque hue, about 25 minutes. Remove from the oven and let cool on the baking sheet for 10 minutes.

Using a sharp knife, cut each log on the diagonal into slices about ½ inch thick. Place the slices, cut side down, on the baking sheet. Bake the cookies until tawny, 7 or 8 minutes longer, then remove from the oven. Turn the pieces over and bake on the other side until faintly golden, another 7 or 8 minutes. Transfer the *biscotti* to racks to cool. Store in a tightly covered container for up to 1 week.

MAKES 20 TO 25 BISCOTTI

Mushrooms, cherry tomatoes, baby squashes, and onions all make bite-sized appetizers when stuffed with a savory herbed sausage stuffing, baked, and then served either warm or at room temperature. Any one vegetable might be used, or as here, a colorful combination of four different ones can be prepared. Crisp, dry rosé, dry sherry, and bitter aperitifs such as Suze and *vin de gentaine* are good accompaniments.

6 firm but ripe cherry tomatoes

6 small fresh mushrooms

6 small onions, each approximately 1 inch in diameter

6 baby pattypan or round zucchini squashes, approximately 1 inch in diameter

2 or 3 slices day-old baguette or other sturdy bread

1 cup milk

1 pound bulk sausage

½ teaspoon salt, or to taste

½ teaspoon crushed fennel seeds

1 teaspoon minced fresh thyme

2 tablespoons minced fresh parsley

1 teaspoon freshly ground black pepper

To prepare the tomatoes, squashes, and onions, cut off the tops. Using a small spoon or the tip of a sharp knife scoop out the interiors to make shells with sides about ¼ inch thick. To prepare the mushrooms, remove the stems and then pull away the veil, if any, to expose the cavity.

Preheat an oven to 400 degrees F.

To make the stuffing, in a small bowl, soak the bread in the milk until it is soft, just a few minutes. Squeeze the bread dry and place in a bowl along with the sausage, salt, fennel, thyme, parsley, and pepper. Mix well to form a thick paste. Place a spoonful in each of the vegetable cavities, then mound with another half or full spoonful, according to the size of the vegetable. Remember, each of these should be of a size that can be eaten in a single bite.

Place the stuffed vegetables in a shallow roasting pan just large enough to hold them snugly in a single layer. Place in the oven and bake until the juice of the stuffing runs clear, not pink, about 25 minutes. Remove from the oven and serve warm or at room temperature.

MAKES 4 TO 6 SERVINGS

GRILLED BABY ARTICHOKES

ARTICHOKES ARE CONSIDERED TRICKY TO MATCH WITH BEVERAGES BECAUSE OF THE PRESENCE OF THE NATURAL CHEMICAL *CYNARIN*, WHICH CAUSES A REACTION IN SOME PEOPLE that makes everything taste sweet for a short time. When marinated and then grilled, however, the artichokes take on other flavors as well, here, that of olive oil, herbs, lemon, and, of course, the smokiness from the grill. The young artichokes are thus transformed into Mediterranean *amuse-gueules*, suitable for eating with red wine, *vins maison*, rosé, *pastis*—in short, the flavors of the *terroir*, where they grow in abundance. The baby artichokes are grilled whole, with no initial preparation necessary other than rinsing with water and patting dry. Once grilled, the blackened and charred outer leaves are peeled away to reveal the tender interior leaves and the heart, which have steamed underneath. Serve them with a dip, such as *anchoiade* (page 131), an herb-seasoned butter, or mayonnaise, or offer them plain.

½ cup olive oil

zest of 1 lemon, coarsely chopped

½ cup medium-dry white wine such as Chenin Blanc or dry vermouth

¼ cup fresh marjoram leaves, or 6 to 8 marjoram stems

¼ cup fresh lemon thyme leaves, or 8 to 10 lemon thyme stems

¼ cup chopped fresh parsley

1 teaspoon salt

1 tablespoon cracked black pepper

12 baby artichokes, 2 or 3 ounces each

Combine all the ingredients except the artichokes in a large glass bowl, mixing well. Add the artichokes, turning to coat them with the marinade. Let them marinate for at least 4 hours or as long as 12 hours, turning them often.

Prepare a fire in a charcoal (or gas) grill, preferably with a cover. When the fire is ready, place the artichokes on the grill rack about 8 inches above the heat and cover, making sure the air holes are open, and cook for 10 minutes. Remove the cover, turn the artichokes, and continue to grill until the artichokes are tender and easily pierced with the tip of a sharp knife, another 5 to 10 minutes.

If you are not using a covered grill, cook the artichokes on a grill rack about 10 inches above the fire, turning them often and watching them to make sure they are charring yet cooking evenly. Test for doneness by piercing with the tip of a sharp knife. They should be ready in about 15 or 20 minutes.

Remove the artichokes and let them stand for 5 minutes before serving, or serve them warm or at room temperature. MAKES 4 TO 6 SERVINGS

WILD MUSHROOM AND GOAT CHEESE GALETTES

*T*HESE ARE A SPECIALTY OF GERALD HIRIGOYEN, CHEF-OWNER OF FRINGALE AND PASTIS RESTAURANTS IN SAN FRANCISCO. HE MAKES THEM USING THICK, DEEP-FRIED POTATO RINGS instead of pastry for the *galettes,* and he fills the rings with a delectable mixture of various mushrooms and goat cheese. The surface is then smoothed and coated with bread crumbs and the filled *galettes* are briefly sautéed to a golden brown and served immediately, a fine appetizer to accompany any aperitif.

peanut or vegetable oil for deep-frying

2 large russet potatoes, well scrubbed

❋

For the mushroom filling:

3 ounces fresh shiitake mushrooms

3 ounces fresh morel mushrooms

3 ounces fresh chanterelle mushrooms

3 ounces fresh oyster mushrooms

1 tablespoon minced shallots

2 tablespoons olive oil

1 clove garlic, minced

½ teaspoon salt

¼ teaspoon white pepper

2 ounces fresh goat cheese

1 egg

1 tablespoon chopped fresh parsley

1 tablespoon chopped fresh chives

❋

2 heaping tablespoons fine dried bread crumbs

1 tablespoon olive oil

½ tablespoon chopped fresh parsley

freshly ground black pepper

In a deep-fat fryer or heavy-bottomed saucepan, pour in the peanut or vegetable oil to a depth of 3 inches. Heat to approximately 300 degrees F on a deep-frying thermometer, or until a drop of water added to the oil dances and pops on the surface.

Meanwhile, cut off the ends of the potatoes and discard. Slice the center of each potato crosswise into 2 disks each ¾ inch wide. Cut a hole out in the middle of each potato disk, forming a sturdy "ring." (Be sure to leave a ring of at least 1½ inches of potato around each hole.) When the oil is ready, slip the potato rings, a few at a time, into the pan and deep-fry until they start to turn golden brown, about 5 minutes. Using a slotted spoon, remove the potato rings from the oil and place them on paper towels. Pat the rings dry with paper towels, removing any excess oil.

To prepare the mushroom filling, clean all of the mushrooms with a soft brush or damp towels. (If they are very dirty, soak them *briefly* in a bowl of water, lift them out of the water, and gently wipe dry with a soft cloth.) Remove and discard the stems from the shiitake and morel mushrooms. Finely chop all of the mushrooms, toss them together, and set aside.

In a sauté pan over medium heat, combine the shallots and 2

tablespoons olive oil and sauté until just translucent, about 1 minute. Add the garlic and sauté until it begins to soften, another 30 seconds to 1 minute. Then add all of the mushrooms, the salt, and the white pepper. Continue to sauté until all of the mushrooms are cooked through and slightly caramelized, 3 or 4 minutes. Transfer to a bowl and set in a refrigerator to cool completely, 10 or 15 minutes.

In a mixing bowl, thoroughly combine the goat cheese, egg, mushrooms, parsley, and chives. Fill the center of each of the 4 rings with one-fourth of the mushroom–goat cheese mixture. Smooth the surface of each ring by carefully scraping off any protruding stuffing.

Evenly coat both sides of all 4 rings with the bread crumbs. Place the coated rings in a single layer on a clean plate, cover with plastic wrap, and refrigerate for at least 2 hours or for up to 1 day.

Just before serving, warm the 1 tablespoon olive oil in a large nonstick sauté pan over medium heat. Add the potato rings and cook, turning once, just until golden brown on both sides, 20 to 30 seconds on each side.

To serve, transfer the potato rings to 4 individual plates. Scatter some of the ½ tablespoon parsley on the center of each potato ring and sprinkle the plates with the remaining parsley. Add a few turns of black pepper to taste and serve immediately.

MAKES 4 SERVINGS

FOIE GRAS POACHED IN SWEET WINE

*T*HIS RECIPE, ANOTHER DEVELOPED BY CHEF GERALD HIRIGOYEN, IS TRULY SUBLIME. PREPARE IT FOR A SPECIAL APERITIF OCCASION AND SERVE IT WITH CHAMPAGNE OR A *MÉTHODE champenoise* sparkling wine, or with Sauternes or Barsac, as he does at Fringale. The foie gras is marinated and then wrapped in cheesecloth and tied with string before it is poached. Once cooked, it is chilled in the poaching juices for twenty-four hours or more, before being sliced into creamy medallions and served with toasts.

1 fresh foie gras, approximately 1½ pounds

1⅔ cups late-harvest sweet wine such as Barsac or Sauternes

2 teaspoons plus 1 tablespoon salt

2 teaspoons white pepper

7 cups veal stock

ice cubes

1 day-old baguette

Spilt apart the 2 lobes of foie gras and, using a small, sharp knife, remove any thick portions of the veinlike connective tissue running through the lobes. Place the lobes in a dish and pour ⅔ cup of the sweet wine over them. Sprinkle each lobe evenly on all sides with the 2 teaspoons salt and 1 teaspoon of the white pepper. Cover with plastic wrap and let marinate in the refrigerator for 2 to 6 hours (the longer, the better), turning the lobes at least 2 or 3 times to ensure that they are evenly flavored.

Remove the foie gras lobes from the marinade, reserving the marinade, and place them in the center of a large piece of cheesecloth. Wrap the cloth around the lobes and press them gently into a sausage shape. Using kitchen string, securely tie the cheesecloth-wrapped "roll" of foie gras at both ends. Then tie at 1½-inch intervals along the length of the roll, forming a sausage shape 7 or 8 inches long and 2 to 2½ inches wide.

In a saucepan, combine the veal stock, the remaining 1 cup wine, and the reserved marinade. Bring to a boil over medium-high heat and add the 1 tablespoon salt and the remaining 1 teaspoon white pepper. Gently drop the wrapped roll into the liquid. Return to a boil. Poach gently until barely tender to the touch, 4 or 5 minutes.

Meanwhile, select a bowl large enough to hold the roll and fill it with ice cubes, then add a splash of water. When the foie gras is done, using tongs, remove it from the pan and promptly bury it in the bowl of ice to halt the cooking. Let stand for 1 minute, then remove the roll and place it in a deep rectangular terrine or bowl.

Place the saucepan holding the cooking liquid in the bowl of ice to cool it down completely, about 15 minutes. Pour the cooled liquid into the terrine or bowl to cover the roll completely. Cover and refrigerate for at least 24 hours or for up to 3 days.

Just before serving, cut the baguette crosswise into thin slices and toast on both sides until golden. Remove the roll from the stock, snip off the strings, and remove the cheesecloth. To serve, dip a sharp knife into hot water to heat it, wipe the blade dry, and then slice the foie gras into medallions ¼ inch thick. Arrange on a platter or individual plates with the toasted bread slices and serve.

MAKES 10 TO 12 SERVINGS

GARLIC SAUTÉED CLAMS

*T*INY CLAMS NOT MUCH LARGER THAN THE NAIL OF A LITTLE FINGER ARE FOUND ON A STRETCH OF SANDY BEACH ALONG THE MEDITERRANEAN AT LES SAINTES MARIES DE LA MER, not far from Arles. These little clams, called *tellines*, are a regional aperitif tradition at cafés and homes throughout the area. Sautéed in olive oil with garlic and parsley just long enough to pop them open, they make convivial finger food, and the petite bites of seasoned clams certainly pique the appetite. Similar small clams and mussels may be prepared in the same way. Any of the *vins maison* or classic aperitifs are suitable partners, plus either shellfish is especially good, I think, with a glass of chilled Provençal rosé wine.

1 pound small clams or mussels

¼ cup olive oil

4 cloves garlic, minced

¼ cup minced fresh parsley

Wash the clams thoroughly under running water to remove any grit, sand, or dirt. Discard any that do not close when touched. Clean the mussels in the same way, plus, using scissors, clip any beards that are evident. Roughly dry the shellfish with a towel.

In a skillet large enough to hold all the clams or mussels at one time in a near-single layer, warm the olive oil over medium heat. Add the garlic and sauté for a minute or two, stirring, but do not let the garlic brown. Add the clams or mussels to the pan and turn them with a wooden spoon, coating them with the olive oil. Sprinkle on the parsley and cook, shaking the pan and stirring, just until the shells open, 2 or 3 minutes. Serve immediately.

MAKES 3 OR 4 SERVINGS

RISOTTO CROQUETTES

CRUNCHY ON THE OUTSIDE AND CREAMY ON THE INSIDE, THESE ARE BITE-SIZED VERSIONS OF POPULAR ITALIAN AND FRENCH PREPARATIONS COMMONLY MADE FROM LEFTOVER RISOTTO. For a special occasion, however, it is worth stirring up a fresh pot of rice to prepare these tasty appetizers. About half an hour is required for the rice to absorb the broth and the whole to become creamy. *Vin chaud, vins maison, pastis,* and tomato juice are all appropriate to serve.

3 cups chicken stock

2 cups water

3 tablespoons butter

2 tablespoons olive oil

½ yellow onion, minced

2 cups Arborio rice

½ cup chopped cooked artichoke hearts or mushrooms (optional)

1 teaspoon freshly ground pepper

1 teaspoon chopped winter savory or fresh thyme

¼ cup finely grated Parmesan cheese

salt

canola or other light oil for frying

½ cup fine dried bread crumbs

Combine the stock and water in a saucepan and bring to a simmer; keep hot. In another saucepan over medium heat, warm the butter and olive oil together until foamy. Add the onion and sauté until translucent, 2 to 3 minutes. Add the rice and turn it in the oil and butter until it is shiny, a minute or two. Add the artichokes hearts or mushrooms, if using, and the pepper and savory or thyme. Stir to mix well. Now pour in about one-third of the hot liquid and cook over medium heat, stirring constantly as the rice absorbs the stock. As the first addition of liquid is nearly absorbed, add about ¼ cup more hot liquid, and continue to cook, stirring constantly. Add the remaining liquid in two or three additions, again stirring constantly with each addition until nearly absorbed. When nearly all of the liquid has been absorbed, after about 25 minutes, taste the rice. The center of a kernel should offer scant resistance. Finally, stir in the cheese and cook another 2 or 3 minutes, just until the cheese has blended into the whole. Adjust for salt. If you can resist eating it now, spread the risotto on a buttered platter to cool.

Shape the cooled risotto into patties, about 1½ inches in diameter and ½ inch thick and place on waxed paper.

Coat a large skillet with a thin layer of the canola oil and place over medium heat. Meanwhile, spread the bread crumbs and herbs on a sheet of waxed paper or a large plate. Gently press a risotto patty into the bread crumbs, first on one side, then the other. Repeat until all are done. Working in batches, fry the patties in the hot skillet, turning once, until they are lightly browned and hot all the way through, about 1 minute on each side. Remove to a plate or platter lined with paper towels to drain.

Serve the croquettes immediately or at room temperature.

MAKES APPROXIMATELY 25 PATTIES, 8 SERVINGS

MARINATED GOAT CHEESE

*I*N FRANCE ONE CAN BUY JARS OF SMALL GOAT CHEESES PACKED IN A MARINADE OF OLIVE OIL, PEPPERCORNS, AND *HERBES DE PROVENCE*. WHEN SPREAD ON A PIECE OF PLAIN OR GRILLED bread, these cheeses, each about the size of a walnut, make an ideal nibble to accompany aperitifs of all kinds.

Although we don't easily find these *apero*-sized cheeses, the same effect may be accomplished by marinating larger goat cheeses, then cutting them into smaller portions to serve. The goat cheeses that are vacuum packed in plastic are not suitable for this, as they tend to disintegrate in the marinade. Instead, seek out individual cheeses that have received some air curing and have formed a rind, sometimes called bloom. They are commonly found at farmers' markets, cheese shops, and grocers who stock specialty cheeses.

4 fresh goat cheeses with rind, 2 ounces each

1 cup cold-pressed extra-virgin olive oil

10 whole peppercorns

1 dried or fresh rosemary sprig

1 small dried red chili such as árbol

Place the goat cheeses in a clean, dry widemouthed jar that has been sterilized. Pour the olive oil over them and add the peppercorns, rosemary, and chili. Cover and store in a cool, dark place or in the refrigerator. Let marinate for at least 2 weeks or for up to 1 month before serving. At that time, you may wish to remove the chili.

When ready to serve, let stand at room temperature to decongeal the oil. The marinated cheeses will keep in the refrigerator for up to 4 months.

EACH CHEESE YIELDS 4 SERVINGS

BRANDADE OF SALT COD

*T*HERE ARE MANY VERSIONS OF *BRANDADE* OF SALT COD — A THICK SPREAD — AND SOME HAVE A STRONGER FISH FLAVOR THAN OTHERS. IN THIS RECIPE, THE SPREAD IS LIGHT AND FLUFFY because the cod has been combined with mashed potatoes. This is a wonderful topping for toasts. A more elegant use of this Provençal classic is as a filling for *gougères*. This recipe is sufficient to stuff two dozen of the pastries (see page 111).

¾ pound salt cod fillet

2 or 3 leeks, chopped and steamed to make 2 cups

2 or 3 potatoes, boiled, peeled, and coarsely mashed to make 2 cups

cloves from 2 heads of roasted garlic

½ to ⅔ cup olive oil

1 teaspoon white pepper

¼ cup heavy cream

¼ cup milk

mixed young salad greens (optional)

1 or 2 baguettes, cut on the diagonal into slices, about ½ inch thick to make 24 slices

To refresh the salt cod, soak it in several changes of cold water to remove the salt and to reconstitute the fish, making it supple. This may take as little as 2 or 3 hours, or as long as 24 hours. As the saltiness and dryness of salt cod can vary considerably, taste during the refreshing process by cutting off a small piece and cooking it briefly in hot water. Taste for salt. The fish should not be bland, but still taste of salt — although not too much.

Preheat an oven to 350 degrees F. Bring a saucepan of water to a boil. Reduce the heat to a very gentle simmer, add the cod, and poach until the fish flakes easily, 4 to 5 minutes. Do not allow the cod to boil or overcook it as it will become tough. Remove from the water and drain. Let cool, then squeeze dry. Cut into pieces and remove any errant bones. In a food processor or blender, combine the leeks, potatoes, cod, and garlic. Process while adding ⅓ cup olive oil in a thin stream, continuing to blend until a thick, sticky paste forms, 1 to 2 minutes. Add the pepper, cream, and milk and blend just long enough to form a fluffy spread, 30 to 40 seconds longer. Set aside.

Brush both sides of the baguette slices with the remaining olive oil, using only as much as is needed to coat them lightly. Toast them in the oven turning once or twice, until slightly golden, 10 or 15 minutes.

Preheat a broiler. Spread the toasts with the *brandade* and place them under the broiler just long enough to warm and brown the spread, 30 to 40 seconds. Arrange on a tray or on individual plates and garnish with salad greens, if desired. Serve hot.

MAKES 24 TOASTS, 6 TO 8 SERVINGS

ONION CONFIT

ONION *CONFIT*, THICK, GOLDEN BROWN AND LACED WITH FLAVOR, IS A MELTINGLY TENDER SPREAD INFUSED WITH HERBS. USE ONION *CONFIT* ON ITS OWN OR IN COMBINATION WITH FRESH goat cheese. This recipe yields enough *confit* for a dozen baguette toasts. Preheat an oven to 300 degrees F. Cut the butter into several pieces and place it in a shallow baking dish large enough to hold the onions eventually in a heaping layer 1 to 1½ inches deep. Put the baking dish in the oven to melt the butter. Remove the dish and place the sliced onions in it. Sprinkle the herbs, salt, pepper, and sugar evenly over the onions. Drizzle with the olive oil.

Return the dish to the oven and bake, turning the onions in the oil and butter every 10 or 15 minutes, until the onions have turned a light golden brown and have reduced in volume by nearly half, 1 to 1½ hours. Remove from the oven and serve immediately or at room temperature. The *confit* can be covered and stored in the refrigerator for up to 1 week.

3 tablespoons unsalted butter

1½ to 2 pounds yellow onions, sliced ¼ to ⅜ inch thick

2 tablespoons olive oil

½ dried bay leaf

1 teaspoon fresh thyme leaves and 1 teaspoon fresh winter savory leaves

½ teaspoon salt

½ teaspoon freshly ground black pepper

½ teaspoon granulated sugar

MAKES APPROXIMATELY 1 CUP

ANCHOIADE WITH VEGETABLES

FOR LOVERS OF SALT AND THE SEA, OF STRONG, UNCOMPROMISING FLAVORS, ANCHOVIES REIGN SUPREME. THE ANCHOVY IS TYPICALLY PACKED IN SALT OR IN OLIVE OIL, EITHER IN TINS OR glass or ceramic jars, and then used in any number of preparations, the purest of which is an *anchoiade*. No room for compromising the power of the anchovy here. Made into a thick pomade whose only other ingredients are garlic and olive oil, the *anchoiade* is used as a sauce into which raw vegetables are dipped or as a spread for toasts. The saltiness finds a match in all but the most delicate aperitifs, with such robust choices as *vin d'orange*, pineapple slush, sweet vermouth, *vin marquis*, and the Mediterranean's *pastis*.

⅓ to ½ cup extra-virgin olive oil

2 tins (2 ounces each) olive oil–packed anchovy fillets, drained, or 8 whole salt-packed anchovies, filleted and rinsed

2 cloves garlic, mashed and minced

1 black radish, trimmed

1 fennel bulb, trimmed

2 or 3 carrots, peeled

1 bunch red radishes, trimmed

Place the olive oil in a small skillet and warm it over low heat. Add the anchovies and garlic and cook until the anchovies "melt," or dissolve into the olive oil. If you like, help this process along by mashing the fillets with a wooden spoon to achieve a rather thin paste. Alternatively, with a mortar and pestle or in a small food processor, crush the anchovies and garlic together to make a paste. Gradually add olive oil to achieve the desired consistency and intensity. The more olive oil used, the thinner the consistency and less intense the anchovy taste. Start with ⅓ cup oil and add more to taste, up to ½ cup. Transfer the *anchoiade* to a bowl.

Cut the black radish crosswise into ¼-inch-thick slices. Cut the fennel bulb in half lengthwise, then cut each half lengthwise into ¼-inch-thick slices. Cut the carrots into slender 2-inch sticks, but leave the red radishes whole. Arrange the vegetables on a tray with the bowl of *anchoiade* in the center.

MAKES 4 SERVINGS

ACKNOWLEDGMENTS

THIS BOOK COULD NOT HAVE BEEN ACCOMPLISHED WITHOUT THE HELP AND ENTHUSIASM OF MANY PEOPLE, BOTH HERE AND IN FRANCE. FRIENDS LOANED US THEIR HOMES, FLUNG OPEN their pantries and linen closets, unpacked their collections of antiques, and ransacked their gardens for flowers. Hotel, café, and restaurant owners welcomed us into their domains and allowed us full rein, as well as made suggestions from their store of knowledge. Winemakers, aperitif producers, importers, and merchants generously supplied us with detailed information, histories, and samples of their wares.

So thank you all, from Georgeanne, Kathryn, and Ethel, for making this book with us.

Gerald Hirigoyen, chef-owner of the Fringale and Pastis restaurants in San Francisco, who welcomed us with foie gras poached in sweet wine and wild mushroom and goat cheese *galettes* for our camera, and then, once the photography was concluded, fed us a wonderful lunch. Cameron Hirigoyen was ever so helpful during our visit, answering all sorts of questions we posed.

Martyn James, the charming bartender at Fringale, who shared his love of Picon punch, his extensive knowledge, and a glass of sherry.

Steve and Beth Simmons of Bubba's Diner in San Anselmo, California, who let us photograph in their cozy restaurant and who prepared slushes and juices.

Kako Vaugh, owner of the Auberge Rose in Moustiers Ste.-Marie, France, who turned us loose in the splendid zinc bar of his *auberge*, replete with banquettes and tables rescued from a classic turn-of-the-century bar on the Canebière in Marseilles.

Danielle and Deny Berne, proprietors of the family-run Hotel-Restaurant Relais Notre-Dame in Quinson, France, deep in the heartland of Provence, who one day set for us an aperitif table in the garden, laden with an onion tart fresh from the oven and an array of aperitifs from the restaurant's bar, and the next day welcomed us to their outdoor stone sink to photograph the washing of antique bottles, in preparation for *vins maison*.

Jean-Pierre Moullé, downstairs chef at Chez Panisse in Berkeley, California, who shared his philosophy of and interest in *vins maison* and the entire notion of *l'apéritif.*

Paul Bertolli, chef and co-owner of Oliveto restaurant in Oakland, California, who discussed his views and passions for aperitifs.

Catherine Brandel, chef-instructor at the Greystone Culinary Academy in St. Helena, California, a longtime compatriot in the food and farm world, and an aficionado of the aperitif, who generously imparted her expertise on many subjects.

Anne Roussel of Roussel Gallery in Greoux-les-Bain and Pierre Leroux, who so kindly let us photograph at their house set amid the red poppy fields on the Plateau of Valensole.

Brigitte Coirier, artist, and her husband, architect Nicolas Vincent, who were assistants par excellence as they guided us around Uzes, brought us props, and who were especially helpful as we photographed at the chateau of Nicolas's mother, Mme Vincent.

Mme Vincent of Uzes, who not only allowed us to photograph in her home, but also brought her family's collection of silver, glass, linens, dishes, and albums for us to use, as well as gave us rose shears to cut whatever we wanted from her garden.

Mlle Françoise Lamy, who brought *tellines* fresh from the Mediterranean, and cooked them for us in the kitchen of M. and Mme Robert Lamy, explaining aperitif traditions of Arles and elsewhere in the Midi as she did so.

Mme Lamy, neighbor and friend, who has always been an inspiration, never failing to offer one of her many *vins maison* at aperitif time (and for photography), and always willing to spend time answering questions.

Michele Fine and Serge Sabotier, artists and *antiquaires* of Montagnac, who unpacked cartons and trunks and armoires of antique tableware and linens, old family portraits, frames, and artifacts for our perusal and use. They opened their huge stone house, its gallery and its gardens to us, wove flower garlands and ironed cloths for photography, and assisted over several days in every gracious way. Michele, too, loaned his mother's old recipe book, and we all sampled her *vin marquis*.

Georgina and Denys Fine, artists of Moustiers Ste.-Marie, old and dear friends, who as always were enthusiastic and willing to help in every way, from collecting and writing out family recipes to doing calligraphy on labels to polishing their collection of nineteenth-century bistro glasses and bottles. They opened their ancient house and its stone terraces and hidden gardens for photography and kept us well fed as we worked.

Adele and Pascal Degremeont, whose long friendship, support, and knowledge of all things Provençal have contributed over the years to many, many happy and pleasurable moments, meals, aperitifs, and adventures.

Marie and Marcel Palazoli, neighbors and friends, who allowed us to gather at will from their fabled *potager*, to pick all the cherries we wanted, and from whom so much as been learned.

Charlotte Kimball and Tom Neeley, who were always at hand to explore the world of aperitifs.

Linda Thurmond, who so cheerfully allowed herself to be abducted into the work world of photography while on vacation in France.

AT CHRONICLE BOOKS

Our editors, the ever-passionate and enthusiastic Bill LeBlond and Leslie Jonath, who let us shape and develop this book as we chose, to our art director Michael Carabetta and his assistant Julia Flagg for their support, and to Louise Fili and Mary Jane Callister, who brought our vision to life with their design of the book. Finally, to Sharon Silva, the best editor anyone could ever have.

THE FOLLOWING PEOPLE FROM THE COMMERCIAL WORLD OF
WINE, SPIRITS, AND APERITIFS WERE OF GREAT ASSISTANCE TO US

Robert Shack, Director of Fine Wine Sales, Premiere Wine Merchants (A Division of Remy Amerique, Inc.), New York.

Pascal Rolland, Commercial Director, Distilleries et Domaines de Provence, Forcalquier, France.

Bruno-Eugene Borie, President, Lillet Frères, Podensac, France.

Laurent Sarazin, Director, Foods and Wines from France, San Francisco.

Claudine Eynaud, Pernod S.A., Paris.

Barbara Waits, Sager-Bell, Inc, representing Bolla, Fontana Candida, and Fontanafredda Italian wines; Carmen Vineyards in Chile; and Jekel Vineyards in Monterey, California, as well as Noilly-Prat French vermouth.

Hugues Chatelian, Export Director of Ricard, Marseilles, representing Ricard and Dubonnet.

Laura Baddish, The Alden Group, representing Martini & Rossi and Champagne Pommery.

Sterling Vineyards, Napa, California; Tom Ferrell of Spring Mountain Vineyard, St. Helena, California; and Michael Butler of Kermit Lynch, Wine Merchant, Berkeley, California.

SPECIALLY FROM KATHRYN

Many thanks forever to Georgeanne Brennan for allowing me to work on this wonderful project with her. It proved a continual joy because of her talents and of her vision of the subject of the aperitif and its place in our daily lives.

Thanks to Ethel Brennan for her wealth of abilities—location scouting, propping, photography assistance in France, food preparation and styling in the studio—and for her companionship and perpetual optimism, all of which made this project a delightful adventure. Never could we have accomplished so much in so little time without her.

Many thanks to Heidi Arnesen, Teresa Retzlaff, and Kirstie Laird for their managerial skills and for keeping me on track with my life in my photography studio.

Thank you to Erin Toddhunter for her tutoring me in French, for her organizational and production support on this project, and for her devotion to making my life less complicated and more focused in every way. I could not have done this without her.

A thank you to Caroline Kopp, photography assistant extraordinaire, for her faithful support of my work and this project.

Thank you to my guys Eric and Peter for taking care of Daddy while I traveled, and thank you to Margareta and Rosie and Bill, who made their lives more fun.

And thank you to Michael Schwab for his unending love and support of my projects in life.

SPECIALLY FROM GEORGEANNE

Deepest thanks, as always, to my husband, Jim Schrupp, for reading and editing all my words, for sampling food and drink, and for being such a staunch and loving partner.

A special thank you to the wonderful Ethel, who brings so much to this book, and to my life, and to my other three children, Oliver, Tom, and Dan, who continue to enthuse about my projects and to sample my wares with a critical eye and palate.

Thank you, thank you to Kathryn Kleinman, for agreeing to join me in this project. The whole experience of working and traveling together was exhilarating. Her ability to capture the essence of a moment on film, bringing it to life in a most evocative way, makes this book particularly special.

Thank you to my faithful and notable agent, Susan Lescher, and to her very kind and helpful staff, Carolyn Larson, Micky Choate, Barbara Craig, and Richard Prentiss.

MAIL-ORDER SOURCES

If there is no shop that carries wine-making equipment in your
community, call or write the following businesses to order by mail:

Oak Barrel Winecraft

1443 SAN PABLO AVENUE

BERKELEY, CALIFORNIA 94702

TELEPHONE: 510-849-0400

Demptos Glass of California

840 D LATOUR COURT

NAPA, CALIFORNIA 94558

TELEPHONE: 707-224-1000

Association pour la Formation et la Vulgarisation en Milieu Agricole. Les Côtes-du-Rhône: du vigno-
ble à la table. Avignon: AFVMA, 1988.

Biehn, Michel. "Venez donc prendre un verre . . ." *Côté Sud,* no. 29, August—September 1994.

Conrad, Barnaby. *Absinthe: History in a Bottle.* San Francisco: Chronicle Books, 1988.

Delahaye, Marie-Claude. *Le livre du pastis.* Nice: Z'editions, 1994.

Dumay, Raymond. *Guide des alcools.* Nancy: Editions Stock, 1973.

Hirigoyen, Gerald. *Bistro.* Menlo Park, Calif.; Sunset Books, 1995.

Jeffs, Julian. *Sherry.* 4th edition. London: Faber and Faber, 1992.

Lampriere, Denyse. "Xérès, ces arômes flamenco." *Côté Sud,* no. 29, August-September, 1994.

Lynch, Kermit. *Adventures on the Wine Route.* New York: Farrar, Straus and Giroux, 1988.

Parker, Robert M., Jr., *The Wines of the Rhone Valley and Provence.* New York: Simon and Schuster, 1987.

Reboul, J. B., *La cuisinière provençale.* Marseilles: Tacussel, 1910.

Sertl, William. "Good and Bitter." *Saveur,* no. 10, January—February 1996.

Slavin, Sara, and Karl Petzke. *Champagne: The Spirit of Celebration.* San Francisco: Chronicle Books, 1995.

Smith, Michael and Christian Flacelière. "L'amertume se boit glacée." *Saveurs,* no. 41, June 1994.

SOPEXA. *The Wines and Spirits of France.* Paris: SOPEXA, 1989.

TABLE OF EQUIVALENTS

The exact equivalents in the following tables have been rounded for convenience.

US / UK

oz=ounce

lb=pound

in=inch

ft=foot

tbl=tablespoon

fl oz=fluid ounce

qt=quart

METRIC

g=gram

kg=kilogram

mm=millimeter

cm=centimeter

ml=milliliter

l=liter

WEIGHTS

US / UK	METRIC
1 oz	30 g
2 oz	60 g
3 oz	90 g
4 oz (¼ lb)	125 g
5 oz (⅓ lb)	155 g
6 oz	185 g
7 oz	220 g
8 oz (½ lb)	250 g
10 oz	315 g
12 oz (¾ lb)	375 g
14 oz	440 g
16 oz (1 lb)	500 g
1 ½ lb	750 g
2 lb	1 kg
3 lb	1.5 kg

OVEN TEMPERATURES

FAHRENHEIT	CELSIUS	GAS
250	120	½
275	140	1
300	150	2
325	160	3
350	180	4
375	190	5
400	200	6
425	220	7
450	230	8
475	240	9
500	260	10

LIQUIDS

US	METRIC	UK
2 tbl	30 ml	1 fl oz
¼ cup	60 ml	2 fl oz
⅓ cup	80 ml	3 fl oz
½ cup	125 ml	4 fl oz
⅔ cup	160 ml	5 fl oz
¾ cup	180 ml	6 fl oz
1 cup	250 ml	8 fl oz
1 ½ cup	375 ml	12 fl oz
2 cups	500 ml	16 fl oz
4 cups/1 qt 1l		32 fl oz

LENGTH MEASURES

⅛ in	3 mm
¼ in	6 mm
½ in	12 mm
1 in	2.5 cm
2 in	5 cm
3 in	7.5 cm
4 in	10 cm
5 in	13 cm
6 in	15 cm
7 in	18 cm
8 in	20 cm
9 in	23 cm
10 in	25 cm
11 in	28 cm
12 in/1 ft	30 cm